CHARLES BUKOWSKI

BETTING ON THE MUSE

POEMS & STORIES

ecco

An Imprint of HarperCollinsPublishers

BETTING ON THE MUSE: POEMS & STORIES by Charles Bukowski.
Copyright © 1996 by Linda Lee Bukowski.

These poems & stories are part of an archive of unpublished work that Charles
Bukowski left to be published after his death.

ACKNOWLEDGEMNTS

On behalf of the author the publisher would like to thank the editors of the peri-
odicals where some of these poems and stories first appeared.

Cover photograph © by Michael Montfort

First Ecco paperback edition published 2004.

Library of Congress Cataloging-in-publication data

Bukowski, Charles.
    Betting on the muse : pomes & stories / Charles Bukowski.
        p. cm.
    ISBN 1-57423-002-6 (cloth trade: alk. paper).—ISBN 1-57423-001-8

    1. Bukowski, Charles—Literary collections. I. title
PS3552U4B4   1996
811'.54—dc20   96-14678
                                                         CIP

24 25 26 27 28 LBC 25 24 23 22 21

for Linda Lee

TABLE OF CONTENTS

BETTING *on the* MUSE:

POEMS
&
STORIES

splash

the illusion is that you are simply
reading this poem.
the reality is that this is
more than a
poem.
this is a beggar's knife.
this is a tulip.
this is a soldier marching
through Madrid.
this is you on your
death bed.
this is Li Po laughing
underground.
this is not a god-damned
poem.
this is a horse asleep.
a butterfly in
your brain.
this is the devil's
circus.
you are not reading this
on a page.
the page is reading
you.
feel it?
it's like a cobra.
it's a hungry eagle
circling the room.

this is not a poem.
poems are dull,

they make you
sleep.

these words force you
to a new
madness.

you have been blessed,
you have been pushed
into a
blinding area of
light.

the elephant dreams
with you
now.
the curve of space
bends and
laughs.

you can die now.
you can die now as
people were meant to
die:
great,
victorious,
hearing the music,
being the music,
roaring,
roaring,
roaring.

the women

my uncle Ben was interested in the
ladies
and many a time he would drive up
in his Model-A,
get out and come in with his new
lady.
they'd sit on the couch and chatter
away,
then my Uncle Ben would follow
my father into another
room.

"come on, Henry," he'd say to my
father,
"let me have a couple of bucks …"

"you're nothing but a bum," my
father would answer, "get your-
self a job!"

"Henry, I'm trying!
I've been to 6 places already
today!"

"you haven't, you just want
money for that whore!"

the going rate in those days
was two dollars.

"listen, dear brother, I'm
hungry!"

"you're hungry to go to bed
with that whore!
where do you find them
all?"

"shhh ... she's a lady, an
actress!"

"get her out of my house!
we don't allow those kinds
of women in here!"

"Henry, just two bucks ..."

"get her out of here before
I throw her out of
here!"

my uncle would walk back into
the other room.

"come on, Clara, let's go ..."

they would leave the house
together
and we would hear the
Model-A starting up and
driving off.

my mother would run about
opening all the windows
and doors.

"she stinks!
that cheap perfume, that
awful cheap perfume!"

"we're going to have to
fumigate this place!"
my father would scream.

it would be the same
scene over and over
again,
in a few days or a week
the Model-A would pull
up and in would walk
my uncle Ben with
another woman.

"come on, Henry, just
two bucks!"

I never saw my
uncle Ben get his two
bucks
but he tried again and
again.

"those women are so
ugly," my mother would
say.

"I don't know where he
finds them," my father
would say, "and I don't
know where he gets the
gas for his car!"

they would sit down
then and a great gloom
would fall over them
for the remainder of
the day.
they would stop talking
and just sit there,
there would be nothing
else to do
but just sit there
thinking how terrible it
had been—
that woman actually
daring to enter their
lives,
to leave her smell,
and the remembrance
of
her laughter.

the monkey

one summer Saturday afternoon
during the depression
an organ grinder came into the
neighborhood.
he stopped on each
block
and played his organ
and while he played
the monkey did a little
dance.
it was an awkward dance.
the monkey was on a leash
which sometimes hindered
his movements.
but as we watched
it did a little somersault
or stuck its tongue out
at us.
it was dressed in a vest
and pants and had a
little hat strapped to its
head.

when the music stopped
the man gave it a tin
cup
and the monkey went
from person to
person
holding out its
cup.

we children gave it
pennies
but some of the adults
gave it nickels,
dimes and
quarters.
then the man would
take the cup and
empty it of the
money.

the man was fat,
needed a
shave
and wore a red
Sultan's hat
badly faded by
the sun.

the man and the
monkey went from
house to
house.
we followed him.
the monkey had
tiny dark
unhappy
eyes.

then they got to
my father's
house and stood in
the driveway.
the man began to
play his organ
and the monkey

danced.

the door was
flung open and my
father rushed
out.

"what's all the god-
damned noise?"

he stood angrily next to the
man.

"that ape is probably
diseased!
if he shits on my lawn
you clean it
up!"

"he's got a rubber
diaper on,"
said the man,
continuing to
play the
organ.

"that's unnatural!
how'd you like to
wear
rubber
diapers?"

"they'd look better
on you,"
the man said,
continuing to play

the organ
as the monkey
pirouetted,
then did a
flip.

"what did you
say?" my father
asked.

"you heard me,"
said the
man.

"why don't you
get a decent job
and put that stinking
animal in the
zoo?" my father
screamed.

the loud screaming
upset the monkey
and he leaped on
top of the
organ.
he had fang-like
yellow teeth
his lips curled back
and he bit the
organ grinder
on the hand,
hard,
grabbed the tin
cup, leaped to the
cement and began

wildly circling with
it.

the man was bleeding
badly.
he took out a handkerchief
and wrapped it around
his hand.
the blood soaked
through.
the monkey took the
cup and hurled it
into the
street.

the man sighed
heavily.
then carrying the
organ
and dragging the
monkey
he walked out
into the street and
picked up the
cup.

"you stay out of this
neighborhood!"
my father
yelled.

"this is a free
country, I can go
anywhere!"
the man yelled
back.

"yeah?
get your ass out of
here or I'm going to
kick it
out!"

"you and whose
army?" the organ
grinder
asked.

"*my* army! I
served in World War
One!
where were
you?"

the monkey was
straining at the
end of his
leash, pulling
against it,
he was
choking.

the man picked
it up, kissed it,
put it on his
shoulder.

"you've upset
my monkey,"
he said.

"be glad that's
all,"

said my
father.

the organ grinder
walked off
with the monkey
on his
shoulder.

my father walked
back into the
house,
slamming the
door.

we watched
the man and the
monkey.
they reached
the end of
the block.
then they turned
the corner and
were
gone.

we all just stood
there.
nobody said
anything.

then somebody
said, "well, the
monkey's gone,
let's do something
else."

"what?"

"I don't know ..."

there were five of
us.
we turned and
began walking
down the
sidewalk, the
other
way.

something would
turn
up.

she said, "all of a sudden
someone arrived.
he was called just
'Edgar' ...
he was a post-Impression-
ist painter,
dressed all in black.
it was stunning.
he was wearing a black
hat with a large
brim.
he was wearing a
rather high collar and a
lavaliere, the kind
that only artists
wear.
and he had a black
cape, was dressed
like Whistler.

he was probably in his
60s
but he was a most
handsome man.
he was bringing a huge
bouquet—*c'était à la mode
des violettes de Palmes*—
the violets from Palma—
which are pale violets,
and he cut a
fantastic figure."

when everybody left
I said to my grandmother,
"Who was that man?"
and she said, "Ah,
he is an
Artist."

when my grandmother said
that,
she meant *"Ah,
mais oui, c'était une artiste!"*

and I answered right away,
"Ah, moi aussi."

oh, Jesus or somebody
help us, help us, help
us,
save us from
these,
the centuries have
reeked with them.
no wonder the animals
are what we consort
with,
no wonder we sleep
away the
nights.

the pleasures of the damned
are limited to brief moments
of happiness:
like the eyes in the look of a dog,
like a square of wax,
like a fire taking the city hall,
the county,
the continent,
like fire taking the hair
of maidens and monsters;
and hawks buzzing in peach trees,
the sea running between their claws,
Time
drunk and damp,
everything burning,
everything wet,
everything fine.

those marvelous lunches

when I was in grammar school
my parents were
poor
and in my lunch bag there was
only a peanut butter sandwich.

Richardson didn't have a
lunch bag,
he had a lunch pail with
compartments, a
thermos full of
chocolate milk.
he had ham sandwiches,
sliced beef sandwiches,
apples, bananas, a
pickle and a large bag of
potato chips.

I sat next to Richardson
as we ate.
his potato chips looked
so good—
large and crisp as the
sun blazed upon
them.

"you want some potato
chips?" he would
ask.
and each day
I would eat some.

as I went to school each
day
my thoughts
were on Richardson's
lunch, and especially
those chips.

each morning as we
studied in class
I thought about
lunch time.
and sitting next to
Richardson.

Richardson was the
sissy and the other
boys looked down
on me
for eating with
him
but I
didn't care.
it was the potato
chips, I couldn't
help myself.

"you want some
potato chips, Henry?"
he would
ask.

"yes."

the other boys got
after me
when Richardson

wasn't
around.

"hey, who's your
sissy friend?
you one
too?"

I didn't like that
but the potato
chips were more
important.

after a while
nobody spoke to
me.

sometimes I ate
one of Richardson's
apples
or I got half a
pickle.

I was always
hungry.
Richardson was
fat,
he had a big
belly
and fleshy
thighs.
he was the only
friend I had in
grammar
school.
we seldom spoke

to each
other.
we just sat
together at
lunch time.

I walked home with
him after school
and often some of
the boys would
follow us.

they
would gather around
Richardson,
gang up on him,
push him around,
knock him
down
again and
again.

after they were
finished
I would go
pick up his lunch
pail,
which was
spilled on its
side
with the lid
open.

I would place the
thermos back
inside,

close the
lid.

then I would
carry the pail as
I walked Richardson
back to his
house.

we never spoke.

as we got to his door
I would hand him
the lunch
pail.

then the door would
close and he would
be gone.

I was the only friend
he had.

sissies live a hard
life.

panties

hell, I don't know how old I was,
maybe 7,
and Lila lived next door to me,
she was, maybe 6, and one day
she was standing in her yard
and she looked at me
and lifted her dress and showed
me her panties.
something about it looked good
to me and I stared
and then she let her dress
fall back down and she walked
off.
"Lila," I yelled, "come back!"
she didn't.
but thereafter
every day when she
saw me
she would lift her dress and
show me her panties.
they were a nice clean white
and fitted snugly.
then she would let her dress
fall back down and walk off
again.

one day I was in the back
yard and 3 kids
I had never seen before
came running in
and started swinging their

fists at me.
I surprised myself, I
fought back well, in
fact I gave 2 of them
bloody noses and they
ran off.
but the bigger kid
remained and we
kept fighting.
he began to slowly
wear me down.
he backed me up against
the fence
and I was catching
3 punches to each
one I threw.
his hands were much
larger than mine
and he was very
strong.
then there was a
dull thump.
somebody had hit
him over the
head with something,
a large bottle.
it was Lila.
she hit him
again
and he ran from the
yard
yowling and holding
his head.

"thanks, Lila," I said,
"show me your

panties."

"no," she said.

she walked
back to her house
and went inside.

I saw her many times
after that in her
yard.
I'd ask her,
"show me your
panties, Lila."
but she always
said, "no."

then her family
sold their house and
moved away.

I never quite
understood what it all
meant
and still
don't.

the dead flowers of myself

bulls strut in pinwheel glory,
rockets stun the sky,
but I don't know
quite what to make
of the dead flowers
of myself,
whether to dump them
out of the bowl
or
press them between
these blank pages
and go on;
well, all grief comes down
to hard death
and weeping finally ends.
thank the god
who made
it.

when I was a kid
one of the questions asked was,
would you rather eat a bucket of shit
or drink a bucket of piss?
I thought that was easy.
"that's easy," I said, "I'll take the
piss."
"maybe we'll make you do both,"
they told me.
I was the new kid in the
neighborhood.
"oh yeah," I said.
"yeah!" they said.
there were 4 of them.
"yeah," I said, "you and whose
army?"
"we won't need no army," the
biggest one said.
I slammed my fist into his
stomach.
then all 5 of us were down on
the ground fighting.
they got in each other's way
but there were still too many
of them.
I broke free and started
running.
"sissy! sissy!" they yelled.
"going home to mama?"
I kept running.
they were right.

I ran all the way to my house,
up the driveway and onto the
porch and into the
house
where my father was beating
my mother.
she was screaming.
things were broken on the floor.
I charged my father and started swinging.
I reached up but he was too tall,
all I could hit were his
legs.
then there was a flash of red and
purple and green
and I was on the floor.
"you little prick!" my father said,
"you stay out of this!"
"don't you hit my boy!" my mother
screamed.
but I felt good because my father
was no longer hitting my
mother.
to make sure, I got up and charged
him again, swinging.
there was another flash of colors
and I was on the floor
again.
when I got up again
my father was sitting in one chair
and my mother was sitting in
another chair
and they both just sat there
looking at me.
I walked down the hall and into
my bedroom and sat on the
bed.

I listened to make sure there
weren't any more sounds of
beating or screaming
out there.
there weren't.
then I didn't know what to
do.
it wasn't any good outside
and it wasn't any good
inside.
so I just sat there.
then I saw a spider making a web
in the window.
I found a match, walked over,
lit it and burned the spider.
then I felt better.
much better.

the snails

my mother stood at the
window
watching my father
in the back
yard.
he was bent over in the
flower garden,
very still, very
intense.

"what's he doing out
there?" my mother
asked me.

"I don't know."

"look, he hasn't moved,
he's like a
statue!"

"yes."

"I'm going to see what
he's doing!"

I watched her walk out
into the yard,
she walked up very
quietly
behind him.

then she screamed.

she came running
into the house,
screaming,
"my god, my god,
my god!"

"what's wrong?"
I asked.

"What's wrong?
What's wrong?
He was watching
two snails doing it
to each other!"

she screamed a long
and horrible scream.
the tears were rolling
down her face.

my father walked in.
"oh, shut up!"
he said.

"Why did you do
that?
Why did you watch?"

"I told you to shut up!"

I walked out of the room
and into the
bedroom and closed the
door.

I could still hear them
screaming,
it went on and on.
then there was the sound
of
breaking glass,
then the slamming of a
door.

I walked out into the front
room.
my mother was sitting on
the couch,
the tears were still running
down her face.

she looked at me.
"why did he do that?
my god, why did he do
that?"

"I don't know," I told
her.

then I turned and
walked back to the
bedroom.

again

now the territory is taken,
the sacrificial lambs have been slain,
as history is scratched again on the sallow walls,
as the bankers scurry to survive,
as the young girls paint their hungry lips,
as the dogs sleep in temporary peace,
as the shadow gets ready to fall,
as the oceans gobble the poisons of man,
as heaven and hell dance in the anteroom,
it's begin again and go again,
it's bake the apple,
buy the car,
mow the lawn,
pay the tax,
hang the toilet paper,
clip the nails,
listen to the crickets,
blow up the balloons,
drink the orange juice,
forget the past,
pass the mustard,
pull down the shades,
take the pills,
check the air in the tires,
lace on the gloves,
the bell is ringing,
the pearl is in the oyster,
the rain falls
as the shadow gets ready to fall again.

were best, the aviators drank at the bar
every night, fighting over the one or two blondes,
and it was gallant because in the dawn they
might die going after those Fokkers with their
Spads, so they lined up along that bar
and slugged them down.

we kids loved those movies, the men weren't
like our fathers, those men laughed and fought
and loved slinky blondes in long tight dresses.

each dawn was glorious, they'd go to their Spads,
pulling on their goggles, a quick wave of the hand and
a long white scarf flowing out behind them. They
grinned and flew off into the blue.

and then came the Germans high above the
clouds.
they'd spot the Spads, the leader would give the
signal and they'd dive downward with a roar,
coming down through the clouds, their machine guns
spitting fire,
and the Spads would see them
but not before one of the planes would be hit
and roar down in flames—usually
the guy with the sense of humor, the guy who
had made everybody laugh at the bar—
there he'd go, his hands rising in the
flames, then oil splashing his goggles, he'd
wiggle trying to free himself to parachute to safety
but it was always too late—

you'd see the Spad crash into a hill
exploding in a mass of flame.

the dogfight was a real spectacle, the hero
would have a Fokker on his tail, have to pull
an Immelman to get him off.
then he'd be on the other guy's tail
and the bullets would rip through
the German, his mouth would open, a
spurt of blood and his plane would head
toward the earth with a WHINING roar.

the dogfights were exciting and lasted a
long time but the Germans always lost
and one or two of their remaining planes
would limp off and that would be it.

then the Spads would begin their
journey back to the airfield.
this was always very dramatic because
one or two of them would be shot up,
crippled, being nursed back, often
the pilot hit by 3 or 4 bullets but
determined to bring the plane back
in and land it safely.

the ground crew would be
waiting and they would count the Spads
as they came in: one, two ... 6, 7,
8 ... but there had been ten ...
the ground crew would be
badly shaken.
the crippled planes would come in first,
followed by the
others.

it was a very sad time.

but that night the remaining pilots would
be back at the bar with the slinky blondes,
even the aviators who had been shot were
there.
they had their arms in slings, their heads
bandaged but they were drinking and
making the slinky blondes
laugh.

outside the movie theaters they displayed
parts of a Spad, a huge wing, a
propeller, and at night there was a
searchlight probing the skies, you could
see it for miles.

all we boys loved those World War One
movies
and we built our own balsa wood
model airplanes, Spads and
Fokkers.
most kits cost 25 cents
which was a lot of money in the
1930s but somehow
every kid had his own
plane.

we were in a hurry to grow
up.
we all wanted to be
fighter pilots,
we wanted those slinky
blondes, we wanted to lean
against that bar and gulp
down a straight whiskey

like nothing had
happened.

we had dogfights with our
model planes and they
sometimes developed into
fist fights.
we fought until we were
bloody and
torn.
we fought for our
honor

while
our fathers watched us
and
yawned.

that was one of the popular sayings, I didn't know
    what it
meant, standing on a corner in the mid-thirties
with a cigarette dangling from my mouth like the
tough guys in the movies, scoring for some beer
was the big thing and once in a while
some whiskey but there was no money anywhere
for fathers or sons or anybody and we were all
bluffing, tough, nothing else to be, we stood
around flexing our muscles, getting down to the
beach now and then but the young girls ran with
the rich guys with cars (even in bad times
there were rich guys), kids driving canary yellow
convertibles, pulling up to corners, opening doors,
laughing, I could kick any of that ass but it meant
nothing to the girls, they were off with those richies,
their hair flying in the wind, it was a crappy time
for us, standing there on the street corners, our
cigarettes dangling, nothing to be tough about,
nothing near enough to fight and hating our
fathers who sat in chairs or read newspapers
all day, they couldn't find work, their guts hanging
out and their lives hanging out—dried, dead, use-
less.

dinners of beans and canned meats, still we
grew, inching out of our old clothes, leaving our
homes late at night to stand under street lamps or
sit on park benches sucking at wine, beer, gin,
talking, smoking, going to hell and back in a
buggy carriage.

we were tough with nothing to be tough about,
we were the depression kids
and we swore we'd never be like our fathers
or our fathers' fathers.
we'd break through the crap and the
fakery.

we knew something.
we knew something, sitting in the dark,
drinking and smoking.
it was all a matter of which one of us
got there first.

the ends of our cigarettes glowing in the
dark.
as perfect as we could get.
the laughter like knives cutting the
stupid air.

Los Angeles 1935.

back then, you'd go through stages,
one of them being that you'd get so
deeply tanned it was almost horri-
fying, and you'd lift weights, learn
acrobatic techniques,
and all of this was done with
a demonic zest—it was a matter of
fighting back against the stifling
forces everywhere and you had
huge tanned muscles
and you walked like an ape
trying to hold a load in his buttocks.

when you walked into a room, all
conversation stopped, you looked
dangerous, indeed, and you had a
way of staring at people with an
off-hand disdain, and you were not
the only monster from hell, there
were usually one or two others with
you.

you would walk down the street
as if your very feet could break the
sidewalks.
you would work little routines, like
walking up to a fruit stand with the
clerk watching,
you would pick up an apple with
one hand and crush it,
then smile at him and

replace the crushed apple on the
stack.
you ripped phone books in half,
picked up cars by their front
bumpers.
the stronger you got the more
you wanted to use it.
and you not only had strength
but an ultra-quickness—
you caught flies in mid-flight,
shadow-boxed with frightening
speed—left jab, left jab, zip, zip,
right lead, right hook, left hook,
uppercut, you had a pair of red
boxing gloves and you
laced them on with great calm
as your opponent waited, his
eyes jumping with fear.

that was the first stage, the
other was when you gave it
all up, the muscles shrank,
you paled, slouched,
assuming the worst
posture imaginable, smoking
cigarette after cigarette, cough-
ing, masturbating, drinking
endless coffee and all the
booze you could steal.

you had more friends that
way, now you really looked
dangerous and people hung
on your every word, you were
now the ultimate discontent,
your mind a dirty saber

which cut through all the world's
crap.

you found that this stage
garnered you far more
attention, not only from your
peers but from your
the neighbors, the girls and
the teachers.

you were always in the
principal's office, not because
you had done anything
heinous but because you
looked like you might and,
actually, you felt like you
might.

"It's your ATTITUDE, Mr.
Chinaski, it's horrible, in
and out of class."

"huh?"

"Do you want to
graduate?"

"I dunno ..."

"Don't you care?"

"'bout what?"

"Mr. Chinaski, you will now go
and sit in the phone
booth and you will remain

there
until I tell you to come
out!"

"o.k."

it was his phone booth
torture chamber.

I'd go in there, rack my
knees against one wall,
loll my head back and
pretend to go to
sleep.
it pissed him something
awful.

I graduated, still in the
2nd stage,
and I think that I have
been stuck there
ever
since.

the day you were starving and watching the
swans in the park,
it was truly not a bad day
watching them circle,
it was quiet,
you looked at their feathers, their necks,
their eyes.
for a moment you thought of
catching one, killing it, eating it.
but
you had nothing to cook
one on.
and you knew you couldn't do
it anyway.
there were many things you
couldn't do.
that's why you were starving
in a public park.

then there were voices, a
young lady in her summer
dress, and she was with her
young man and they were
laughing.

you looked at them and made
them dead,
you placed them in their
grave,
you saw their bones,
the skulls.

then you got up from the
grass and left them there with
the swans.

you walked out of the park,
you were on the boulevard,
you began walking,
walking seemed sensible
and it wasn't a bad
day,
just another day,
walking the sidewalk,
the world slanting through
your brain—
a white shot of
light.
being alone you decided, was a
magnificent
miracle.
nothing else made any
sense at
all.

woman on the street

her shoes themselves
would light my room
like many candles.

she walks like all things
shining on glass,
like all things
that make a difference.

she walks away.

CONFESSION OF A COWARD

God, she thought, lying in bed naked and re-reading Alding-
ton's *Portrait of a Genius, But* ..., he's an imposter! Not D. H.
Lawrence, but her husband—Henry—with his bauble of a
belly and all the hair he never combed and the way he stood
around in his shorts, and the way he stood naked before the
window like an Arabian and howled; and he told her that he
was turning into a toad and that he wanted to buy a Buddha
and that he wanted to be old and drown in the sea, and that
he was going to grow a beard and that he felt as if he was
turning into a woman.

And Henry was poor, poor and worthless and miser-
able and sick. And he wanted to join the Mahler Society. His
breath was bad, his father was insane and his mother was
dying of cancer.

And besides all this, the weather was hot, hot as hell.

"I've got a new system," he said. "All I need is four or
five grand. It's a matter of investment. We could travel from
track to track in a trailer."

She felt like saying something blasé like, "We don't
have four or five grand," but it didn't come out. Nothing
came out; all the doors were closed and all the windows
were down, and it was in the middle of the desert—not even
vultures—and they were about to drop the Bomb. She
should have stayed in Texas, she should have stayed with
Papa—this man is a goon, a gunnysack, a gutless no-nothing
in a world of doers. He hides behind symphonies and poetic
fancies; a weak and listless soul.

"Are you going to take me to the museum?" she asked.

"Why?"

"They're having an Art Exhibit."

"I know."

59

"Well, don't you want to see Van Gogh?"

"To *hell* with Van Gogh! What's Van Gogh to me?"

The doors closed again and she couldn't think of an answer.

"I don't like museums," he continued. "I don't like museum-people."

The fan was going but it was a small apartment and the heat held as if enclosed in a kettle.

"In fact," he said, peeling off his T-shirt and standing in just his shorts, "I don't like *any* kind of people."

Amazingly, he had hair on his chest.

"In fact," he continued, pulling his shorts down and over the end of one foot, "I'm going to write a book some day and call it *Confession of a Coward.*"

The doorbell rang like a rape, or the tearing of ripe flesh.

"*Jesus Christ!*" he said like something trapped.

She jumped off the bed, looking very white and un-peeled. Like a candy banana. Aldington and D. H. Lawrence and Taos fell to the floor.

She ran to the closet and began stuffing herself inside the flying cloth of female necessaries.

"Never mind the clothes," he said.

"Aren't you going to answer?"

"No! Why should I?"

It rang again. The sound of the bell entered the room and searched them out, scaled and scalded their skins, pummeled them with crawling eyes.

Then it was silent.

And the feet turned with their sound, turning and guiding some monster, taking it back down the stairwell, one two three, 1, 2, 3; and then gone.

"I wonder," he said, still not moving, "what that was?"

"I don't know," she said, bending double at the waist and pulling her petticoat back over her head.

"Here!" she yelled. "*Here!*" holding her arms out like feelers.

60

He finished yanking the petticoat off over her head with some distaste.

"Why do you women wear this crap?" he asked in a loud voice.

She didn't feel an answer was necessary and went over and pulled Lawrence out from under the bed. Then she got into bed with Lorenzo and her husband sat on the couch.

"They built a little shrine for him," he said.

"*Who?*" she asked irritably.

"Lawrence."

"Oh."

"They have a picture of it in that book."

"Yes, I've seen it."

"Have you ever seen a dog-graveyard?"

"What?"

"A dog-graveyard."

"Well, what about it?"

"They always have flowers. Every dog always has flowers, fresh, all in neat little clusters on each grave. It's enough to make you cry."

She found her place in the book again, like a person searching for solitude in the middle of a lake: *So the bitter months dragged by miserably, accompanied by Lorenzo's tragic feeling of loss, his—*

"I wish I had studied ballet," he said. "I go about all slumped over but that's because my spirit is wilted. I'm really *lithe,* ready to tumble on spring mattresses of some sort. I should have been a frog, at least. You'll see. Someday I'm going to turn into a frog."

Her lake rippled with the irritating breeze: "Well, for heaven's sake, *study* ballet! Go at *night*! Get rid of your *belly*! Leap around! Be a frog!"

"You mean after WORK?" he asked woefully.

"God," she said, "you want everything for nothing." She got up and went to the bathroom and closed the door.

She doesn't understand, he thought, sitting on the couch naked, she doesn't understand that I'm *joking.* She's so god-damned *serious*. Everything I say is supposed to carry truth or tragic import, or insight or something. I've been *through* all that!

He noticed a pencil-scrawled piece of paper, in her handwriting, on the side table. He picked it up:

> *My husband is a poet published along-*
> *side Sartre and Lorca;*
> > *he writes about insanity and Nietzsche*
> *and Lawrence,*
> > *but what has he written about me?*
> > > *she reads the funnies*
> > > *and empties garbage*
> > > *and makes little hats*
> > > *and goes to Mass at 8 AM*
> > *I too am a poet and an artist, some dis-*
> *cerning critics*
> > *say, but my husband wrote about me:*
> > > *she reads the funnies ...*

He heard the toilet flush, and a moment later, out she came.

"I'd like to be a clown in a circus," he greeted her.

She got back on the bed with her book.

"Wouldn't you like to be a tragicomic clown stumbling about with a painted face?" he asked her.

She didn't answer. He picked up the *Racing Form*:

> Power 114 B.g.4, by Cosmic Bomb—
> Pomayya, by Pompey
> Breeder, Brookmeade Stable.
> 1956 12 2 4 1 $12,950
> July 18–Jan 1 1/16 1:45 1/5 ft. 3 122 2
> 1/2 3 2h GuerinE' Alw 86

"I'm going to Caliente next Sunday," he said.

"Good. I'll have Charlotte over. Allen can bring her in the car."

"Do you believe she really got propositioned by the preacher in that movie like she claimed?"

She turned the page of her book.

"God damn you, *answer* me!" he screamed, angry at last.

"What about?"

"Do you think she's a *whore* and making it all up? Do you think we're *all* whores? What are we trying to do, reading all these books? Writing all the poems they send back, and working in some dungeon for nothing because we're not *really* interested in *money*?"

She put the book down and looked back over her shoulder at him. "Well," she said in a low voice, "do you want to give it all up?"

"Give WHAT all up? We don't *have* anything! Or, do you mean Beethoven's *Fifth* or Handel's *Water Music*? Or do you mean the SOUL?"

"Let's not argue. Please. I don't want to argue."

"Well, I want to know what we are trying to do!"

The doorbell rang like all the bells of doom sweeping across the room.

"Shhh," he said, "shhh! Be quiet!"

The doorbell rang again, seeming to say, *I know you are in there, I know you are in there.*

"They know we're in here," she whispered.

"I feel that this is *it*," he said.

"What?"

"Never mind. Just be quiet. Maybe it will go away."

"Isn't it wonderful to have all these friends?" she took up the joke-cudgel.

"No. We have no friends. I tell you, *this* is something else!"

It rang again, very short, flat and spiritless.

"I once tried to make the Olympic swimming team," he said, getting completely off the point.

"You make more ridiculous statements by the minute, Henry."

"Will you get *off* my back? Just for *that*!" he said, raising his voice, "WHO IS IT?"

There was no answer.

Henry rose wide-eyed, as if in a trance, and flung the door open, forgetting his nakedness. He stood there transfixed in thought for some time, but it was obvious to her that nobody was there—in his state of undress there would have been quite a commotion or, at the very least, some sophisticated comment.

Then he closed the door. He had a strange look on his face, a round-eyed almost dull look and he swallowed once as he faced her. His pride, perhaps?

"I've decided," he announced, "that I'm not going to turn into a woman after all."

"Well, that will help matters between us considerably, Henry."

"And I'll even take you to see Van Gogh. No, wait, I'll let *you* take me."

"Either way, dear. It doesn't matter."

"No," he said, "you'll *have* to take me!"

He marched into the bathroom and closed the door.

"Don't you wonder," she said through the door, "who that was?"

"Who what was?"

"Who that was at the door? Twice?"

"Hell," he said, "I *know* who it was."

"Who was it, then?"

"Ha!"

"What?"

"I said, 'Ha!' I'm not telling!"

"Henry, you simply don't know *who* it was, anymore than I do. You're simply being silly again."

"If you promise to take me to see Van Gogh, I'll tell you who was at the door."

"All right," she humored him along, "I promise."

"O.K., it was *me* at the door!"

"*You* at the door?"

"Yes," he laughed a silly little laugh, "*me* looking for *me*! Both times."

"Still playing the clown aren't you, Henry?"

She heard the water running in the basin and knew he was going to shave.

"Are you going to shave, Henry?"

"I've decided against the beard," he answered.

He was boring her again and she simply opened her book at a random page and began reading:

> *You don't want any more of me?*
> *I want us to break off—you be free of me,*
> *I free of you.*
> *And what about these last months?*
> *I don't know. I've not told you anything*
> *but what I thought was true.*
> *Then why are you different now?*
> *I'm not—I'm the same—only I know it's no*
> *good going on.*

She closed the book and thought about Henry. Men were children. You had to humor them. They could take no hurt. It was a thing every woman knew. Henry tried—he was just so—all this playing the clown. All the poor jokes.

She rose from the bed as if in a dream, walked across the floor, opened the door and stared. Against the basin stood a partly soaped shaving brush and his still wet shaving mug. But the water in the basin was cold and at the bottom —against the plug, green and beyond her reach at last and the size of a crumpled glove—stared back the fat, living frog.

the secret

don't worry, nobody has the
beautiful lady, not really, and
nobody has the strange and
hidden power, nobody is
exceptional or wonderful or
magic, they only seem to be.
it's all a trick, an in, a con,
don't buy it, don't believe it.
the world is packed with
billions of people whose lives
and deaths are useless and
when one of these jumps up
and the light of history shines
upon them, forget it, it's not
what it seems, it's just
another act to fool the fools
again.

there are no strong men, there
are no beautiful women.
at least, you can die knowing
this
and you will have
the only possible
victory.

somebody else

he had long thin
arms,
sat always in a
white t-shirt,
no gut at all,
he was in his
mid-40s
cheeks hollowed
in,
an x-con,
he rolled a
cigarette with
one hand,
skin burned
brown,
he had crazy
gray
eyebrows,
never looked
right at
you,
he had no
luck with
women,
was always in
love with some
number
who disdained
him,
he coughed too
often,

talked about
all his terrible
jobs of the
past,
sitting in a
chair
he drank wine
out of tall
water glasses,
preferred port,
said muscatel
made him
crazy.

each time
we drank
it was about the
same ...

"come on, Hank,
let's fight!
you've got guts,
let's fight!"

"I don't want to
fight you,
Lou."

I wasn't afraid
of him.
in fact, he
bored
me.

there wasn't
anybody else

to drink with
in that
hotel
except a lady
I knew down
the
hall.

"you banging
her, Hank?"

"maybe."

"can you fix
me up?"

"I don't think
so."

"come on, Hank,
let's fight!"

"go on, drink
your wine."

"I got in a fight
with a guy once,
we used pick
handles.
he broke my
arm on the
first swing.
I still got him.
I busted him
up
good."

he poured the
wine down.
he always got
sick.
he could seldom
make it to the
hall
bathroom.
he'd let it go
in my
sink.

"all right, Lou,
clean up that
fucking
sink!"

"sorry, Hank,
sorry, I think I
got an
ulcer."

"clean the
sink!"

he was like a
17 year old
boy,
nothing had
developed.
I preferred to
drink
alone
but I didn't want
to hurt his
feelings.

one time
he didn't come
around for a
couple of
nights.
that was all
right but he
owed me
ten bucks
and I needed the
money.

I went down to
his door and
knocked.

no answer.

I pushed the
door open.
he was on the
bed
and the gas
heater was
hissing loudly.
it wasn't lit
and all the
windows
were closed.

I shut the
heater off,
opened the
windows
and stood at the
door

swinging it
back and forth
to get air
into the
room.

then I shook
him.
he was still
alive.
he gave me
a stupid
smile.

"Hank, you
saved my
life!
you saved my
life!"

he sat up
in bed,
put his feet
on the
floor.

"you saved
my life!
you're my
buddy
forever!"

"next time
you want to
kill yourself,
lock your

door."

I walked out
of there
and back to
my room.

then he was
knocking on
my door.

I told him
to come
in.

he sat in
the chair.

"I'm in
love,"
he said.

"yeah?"

"it's the
manager.
you ever notice
her body,
her eyes,
her hair?
and she's
intelligent."

"Lou, you owe
me ten
bucks."

"all I got is
a five."

"let me have
it."

he took a
5 from his
wallet.
that's all that
was in
there.

I took it.

"I wrote her a
long love
letter, 4 pages,
I slipped
it under her
door."

"did you
sign it?"

"no."

"don't worry
about
it."

"all right,
Hank.
but I think
she'll know
it's me.

I'm afraid
to face
her.
you got any
wine?"

"one bottle."

"can I have a
drink?"

I got the bottle
and put the
corkscrew to
the
cork.

Lou sat there
and rolled a
cigarette with
one
hand.

A View from the Quarter, March 12th, 1965:

we are in a terrible hurry to die
as large Negroes break the
pavement
our fingers tremble on dark
coffee cups
as this city
all the cities
lie spread-legged
dipped into with
beak,
I awaken to pull a shade
open
I awaken to black men and
white men and no
men—
they rape everything
they walk into churches and
churches burn down
they pet dogs and dogs heave
yellow saliva and
die

they buy paintings that they
don't understand
they buy women that they
don't understand
they buy everything and
what they can't buy
they kill

their women approach me

they wiggle in the sacrament of
their flesh
they sway before me upon the towers
of their high-heels
the whole sum of them wanting
to make me scream
in some idiot's glory
but I look again
and I know that they are
dead
that it is useless
and I cross the street
to buy a loaf of
bread

at night
the sweetest sound I hear is
the dripping of the
toilet
or some unemployed Jazzman
practicing his runs
a wail of martyrdom to an
always
incomplete
self

we only pretend to live
while we wait on something
we wait on something
and look at diamond wrist watches
through plate glass windows
as a spider sucks the guts out of a
fly
we pay homage to Marshal Foch's
granddaughter bending over a
tub of laundry,

we walk down St. Peter St.
hoping to find a
dime in the gutter

the dogs know us
the dogs know us
best
the Jazzman sends it home to
me through the blue glass of a
4 p.m. Friday
afternoon

he wants me to know how he
feels
as feet run over my
head
as the dead men suck in
spaghetti
as the dead men machinegun the
bridge
and in moments of rest
pray and drink
good scotch

I have watched the artists
rotting in their chairs
while the tourists took pictures
of an old iron railing not yet made
into guns

I have seen you, New Orleans,
I have seen you, New York,
Miami, Philly, Frisco, St. Louie,
L.A., Dago, Houston, and
most of the rest. I have
seen nothing. your best men are
drunks and your worst men are

locking them
up,
your best men are killers and
your worst men are
selling them
bullets

your best men die in alleys
under a sheet of paper
while your worst men
get statues in parks
for pigeons to shit upon for
centuries

the Jazzman stops. My god, it's
quiet, that's all I can say now!
it's quiet. it's quiet. let me think
if I feel like thinking and if
I don't, mama, let me not
think.

       4:26 p.m.
       the Quarter

I look down on the floor—
a beer carton
busted open and empty
says

       "Don't litter!
         Keep America
           Beautiful!"

and like the Jazzman:
don't wanta think
no more.

drink

the saddest bar I was ever
in was in New Orleans,
a place west of Canal
Street.
I still remember the
name of it
but for now
let's just call it Bar
Zero.

it was across from
my room,
a mouse-infested
hole on the
second
floor.

I walked into Bar
Zero one night
around eleven
p.m.
and
asked for a
beer.
it took the bartender
an eternity to get it
to me.
the poor devil had
a club foot.

the people

sat at old round
wooden
tables.
the overhead lights
were glaringly
bright.
I was 20 years old,
not too keen on
living
and the place
immediately
brought me
down.

I looked over
at one table.
a lady was sitting
with 3
men.
the poor dear had
a glass eye.
it was bright green,
no sign of a
pupil.
the glass eye
gleamed silently
in the impossible
light.

the men seemed
almost as
one, they looked
so similar,
they were skeletal
with sagging
almost snow-white

skin.
their toothless mouths
hung open.
one of the men was
a bit younger:
a toothpick hung from
his mouth.
he was the liveliest of
that
group.

at another table
a man sat alone in
pin-striped
coveralls.
his beer glass had
tipped upon its
side.
there was a pool
of beer on the
table.
he was
still, he never
moved.
he didn't appear
to be
breathing.
but
out of each
corner of his mouth
oozed two streams
of spittle.
the new spittle
slowly
ran over the old
spittle which had

dried white.

there was a total
silence.
I gulped my beer
down and ordered
another.

an old black and
white dog
sat in the
corner.
his ribs showed
through
as he continued
to bite at his
body,
he never stopped,
the fleas were
eating him
alive.
his teeth were
gone,
so he just gummed
his flesh,
doing what he
could, a gallant
battle—
you heard the
continuous
sucking,
the only
sound in the
place.

then from somewhere
an old dame

appeared,
straight white
hair,
she was dressed
all in black,
looked a
hundred years
old,
she walked up,
stuck her face
into mine,
"HEY!" she
said.

some speech
at last.

"HEY!"

she attempted to
mount the bar
stool next to
mine,
wheezing.
I helped her up
on the
stool,
asked the barkeep
for two
beers.

she put the glass
to her lips, chugged most
of it down,
the rest running
down her face and

into her black
lap.
she made no
attempt to
dry herself.

I ordered her
another
beer.

then one of the
three men at the
other table began
singing:
*"Somebody bet
on the bob-tailed
nag, I'm gonna
bet on the
grey!"*

he sang the same
line three times,
then
stopped.

I asked for a glass
of wine.
when it finally
arrived
there was
dust floating
on the
top.
I drank it
down.
there was the

faint taste of
turpentine.
I ordered
another.

I drank there a couple
of hours.
nothing really
happened.
the bright lights
remained
bright and the
poor dog
kept
gumming at
himself.

"HEY!" the old dame
would yell
and I'd order her
another
beer.

then I remembered I
had something to
drink in my
room.

I got off my stool
and
walked
out.

I walked across
the street,
went to my room,

found the bottle,
sat in a chair,
in the dark,
drinking
and looking
across the street
and into
the bar.

the old dame
had not moved,
the people at the
tables were as
before
as the dog
continued to
chomp.

I heard the mice
moving around
behind me
in the
dark.

where before
they had always
irritated me
with their bold
sharing of my
space,
I now felt the
sound of them,
the presence
of them
almost
endearing.

I drank
from the
bottle
looking down
at the
bar.

I lived in that
room for two
more months
but only once
went back
to that
place.
as I walked
in
the man was
singing:
"Somebody bet
on the bob-tailed
nag, I'm gonna
bet on the
grey!"
and I turned
around and
walked out
and that was
that.

black and white

I must have checked in drunk
because I awakened in the
morning
in a small bed in an old
hotel room.
I wasn't even sure of the
city.
I walked to the window
and looked down.
I was on one of the
upper floors.
the movement of the
people and the automobiles
down there
almost took on a dream-
like
quality.
I had a suicide complex
or I thought I had
one.
I tried to open the window,
it would make a great
jump
down.
the window wouldn't open,
I'd have to try something
else.

there was a knock on the
door.
"come in," I said.

it was a buxom black
maid.
I was standing in my
underwear.
she didn't say
anything, just went about
changing the
sheets.

"what's a good way to
kill yourself?" I asked
her.

"you want to kill your-
self?" she asked.

"yeah."

"you look like you need
a drink."

"yeah."

"I'll order something," she
said.

she got on the
telephone.
I heard her ordering whiskey
and beer.

"what city is this?"
I asked.

"St. Louis."

"you been working here
long?" I asked.

"2 years ..."

she had a duster.
she was dusting things.
the duster was made up of
black and white
feathers.

"forget that," I said.

"forget what?"

"dusting."

she walked over with the
duster and dusted me
up the front.
then she dusted my
rear.

there was a knock at
the door.
I went to my pants and
got my
wallet.
I opened the door,
got the drinks, tipped
him a dollar.

"you sure this is
St. Louis?" I asked.

she took the tray,
uncapped the
whiskey, poured two glasses,
half full, added seltzer

water.
she uncapped 2 bottles
of beer.
we sat on the edge
of the bed,
clicked glasses, went for
it.

"the first one's best,"
she said.

"damn right ..."

we sat there drinking.

"don't you have to work?"
I asked.

"what do you mean?"

"I mean, the rooms, don't
you have to do the
rooms?"

"they won't fire me.
listen, do you really want to
kill yourself?" she asked.

"I think so."

"you're not sure?"

"sometimes I'm more sure
than other times."

"my sister killed herself."

I poured 2 more drinks.

the clock radio said
10: 37 a.m.

"what do you do?"
she asked.

"I'm unemployed."

"you ever worked?"

"many times."

we sat there drinking.

sometimes she poured,
sometimes I did.

soon it was close to
noon.

we ended up in bed
together.

we must have
slept.
when I awakened it was
evening going into
night.

I saw her getting
dressed.
then she was finished.
she walked to the door,
opened it, then walked

out and was
gone.

I got up and sat in a
chair and looked out the
window.

I watched the headlights
of the tiny cars
moving down
there.

and I still didn't know
what to do with
myself.

and all the snow melted

she was a
German girl with a figure like quicksilver
quick something
anyhow
I'd say, "I want to fuck you"
and she'd smile and say
"So?"
we'd be sitting in some cheap nightclub
and the "So?" meant
go ahead
rip my clothes off now
but you won't do that—
so what are you going to do about it?

dear old Gertrude
a design in Sex
in dear old St. Louis
her quicksilver jumping up and down
inside my god-damned soul.

screwing her was like going to heaven
on a drunken trolley
but first it meant
a walk through the snow
watching her ride those haunches
like all the magic in the universe
on those high heels

and up to her vast bed flocked with the
toy animals—stuffed bears, giraffes, elephants,
        whatever—

all looking at us

and my sweeping them to the floor
and the biggest toy animal of them all
taking over
with those bastards on the rug
with their sawdust hard-ons
and dripping cotton tongues, ah

we rode all the way out and
never came back, really,
any of us.

the legs are gone and the hopes—the lava of outpouring,
and I haven't shaved in sixteen days
but the mailman still makes his rounds and
water still comes out of the faucet and I have a photo of
myself with glazed and milky eyes full of simple music
in golden trunks and 8 oz. gloves when I made the
     semi-finals
only to be taken out by a German brute who should have
     been
locked in a cage for the insane and allowed to drink blood.
Now I am insane and stare at the wallpaper as one would
     stare
at a Dali (he has lost it) or an early Picasso, and I send
the girls out for beer, the old girls who barely bother to wipe
their asses and say, "well, I guess I won't comb my hair
     today;
it might bring me luck." well, anyway, they wash the dishes
     and
chop the wood, and the landlady keeps insisting "let me in,
     I can't
get in, you've got the lock on, and what's all that singing
     and
cussing in there?" but she only wants a piece of ass while
     she pretends
she wants the rent
              but she's not going to get either one of 'em.
meanwhile the skulls of the dead are full of beetles and
     Shakes-
peare and old football scores like S.C. 16, N.D. 14 on a John
Baker field goal.

I can see the fleet from my window, the sails and the guns,
      always
the guns poking their eyes in the sky looking for trouble like
      young
L.A. cops too young to shave, and the younger sailors out
there sex-hungry, trying to act tough, trying to act like men
but really closer to their mother's nipples than to a true
      evalu-
ation of existence. I say god damn it, that
my legs are gone and the outpourings too. inside my brain
they cut and snip and
                         pour oil
to burn and fire out early dreams.
"darling," says one of the girls, "you've got to snap out of it,
we're running out of MONEY. how do you want
your toast?
                    light or dark?"

a woman's a woman, I say, and I put my binoculars between
      her
kneecaps and I can see where
empires have fallen.

I wish I had a brush, some paint, some paint and a brush, I
      say.

"why?" asks one of the
whores.

BECAUSE RATS DON'T LIKE OIL! I scream.

(I can't go on. I don't belong here.) I listen to radio programs
and people's voices talking and I marvel that they can get
      excited
and interested over nothing and I flick out the lights, I
crash out the lights, and I pull the shades down, I

tear the shades down and I light my last cigar imagining
the dreamjump off the Empire State Building
into the thickheaded bullbrained mob with the hard-on
        attitude.
already forgotten are the dead of Normandy, Lincoln's
        stringy beard,
all the bulls that have died to flashing red capes,
all the love that has died in real women and real men
while fools have been elevated to the trumpet's succulent
        sneer
and I have fought red-handed and drunk
in slop-pitted alleys
the bartenders of this rotten land.

and I laugh, I can still laugh, who can't laugh when the
        whole thing
is so ridiculous
                that only the insane, the clowns, the half-wits,
the cheaters, the whores, the horseplayers, the bankrobbers,
        the
poets ... are interesting?

in the dark I hear the hands reaching for the last of my
        money
like mice nibbling at paper, automatic feeders on inbred
helplessness, a false drunken God asleep at the wheel ...
a quarter rolls across the floor, and I remember all the faces
        and
the football heroes, and everything has meaning, and an
        editor
writes me, you are good
                        but
                                you are too emotional
the way to whip life is to quietly frame the agony,
study it and put it to sleep in the abstract.

is there anything less abstract
                        than dying day by day?

The door closes and the last of the great whores are gone
and somehow no matter how they have
killed me, they are all great, and I smoke quietly
thinking of Mexico, the tired horses, of Havana and Spain
and Normandy, of the jabbering insane, of my dear
friends, of no more friends
ever; and the voice of my Mexican buddy saying, "you
        won't die
you won't die in the war, you're too smart, you'll take care
of yourself."

I keep thinking of the bulls. the brave bulls dying every day.
the whores are gone. the bombing has stopped for a minute.

fuck everybody.

A NICKEL

It was a lazy day and a lousy day to work. It seemed that even the spiders hadn't thrown out their webs. And when I finally got to my job down at the railroad yards I found out that shithead Henderson was the new foreman.

I learned that the old Mexican, Al or Abe or somebody, had retired or died or gone insane. Too bad. Now Henderson was boss. The boys were matching pennies down by the barn when Henderson called me over.

"Gaines," he said, "Gaines, I understand you're somewhat of a playboy. Well, that's all right. I don't mind a little horseplay now and then, but we'll get our work done first and then we'll play."

"Just like recess at school, eh coach?"

Henderson put his face real close to mine. I put mine real close to his—

"Or haven't you *been* to school, Hendy?"

I could look right down into his red mouth and his frog jaws as he spoke: "I can tie the can to you, boy."

"Proving what?" I asked.

"Proving you are out of position."

Which was a pretty good answer, and a pretty good criticism: I was always out of position.

I took a nickel out of my pocket and flipped it to the cement where the boys were lagging to the line. They stood back stunned, looking from the nickel back to me. I turned around and walked the hell out of there. For good.

II.

I laid up in my room and studied the *Racing Form* for a couple of hours and knocked off half a bottle of left-over wine. Then I got into my 1958 Ford and headed for the track.

I wrote the morning line down on my program and walked over to the bar where I noticed a big blonde, about 35 and alone—well, about as alone as a big babe like that can get amongst 8,000 men. She was trying her damnedest to burst and pop out of her clothes, and you stood there watching her, wondering which part would pop out first. It was sheer madness, and every time she moved you could feel the electricity running up the steel girders. And perched on top of all this madness was a face that really had some type of royalty in it. I mean, there was a kind of stateliness, like she was beyond it all. I mean, there are some women who could simply make damned fools out of men without making any type of statement, or movement, or demand—they could simply stand there and the men would simply feel like damned fools and that was all there was to it. This was one of those women.

I looked up from my drink as if it didn't matter and as if she was just anybody, and as if I was a pretty jaded type (which, to tell the truth, I was) and said, "How you been doin', with the ponies, I mean?"

"All right," she said.

I'd expected something else. I don't know what. But the "all right" sounded good enough.

I was about half-gone on the liquor and felt I owned the world, including the blonde.

"I used to be a jockey," I told her.

"You're pretty big for a jock."

"210, solid muscle," I said.

"And belly," she said, looking right above my belt.

We both kind of laughed and I move closer.

"You want the winner of the first race? To kinda start you off right?"

102

"Sure," she said, "sure," and I felt that big hip-flank touch the side of my leg and I felt like I was on fire.

I smelled perfume, and imagined waterfalls and forests and throwing scraps of venison to fine dogs, and furniture soft as clouds and never again awakening to an alarm clock.

I drained my drink. "Try six," I said. "Number six: *Cat's Head*."

"*Cat's Head*?"

Just then somebody tapped me, I should say—rapped me hard on one of my shoulder blades.

"*Boy,*" the voice said, "*get lost!*"

I stared down into my drink waiting for her to send this stranger away.

"I *said*," the voice got a little louder, "run along and play with your marbles!"

As I stared down into my drink I realized the glass was empty.

"I don't like to play marbles," I told the voice.

I motioned to the bartender. "Two more—for the lady and myself."

I felt it in my back then: what seemed to be the sure, superior nudge of a no doubt highly efficient switchblade.

"Learn," said the voice, "learn to *like* to play marbles!"

"I'm going right away," I said. "I brought my agate. I hear there's a big game under the grandstand."

I turned and caught a look at him as he slid into my seat. And I'd always thought *I* was the meanest-looking-son-of-a-bitch in the world.

"Tommy," I heard her tell him, "I want you to play a hundred on the nose for me."

"Sure. On who?"

"Number six."

"Number SIX?"

"Yes, six."

"But that stiff is 10 to 1!"

"Play it."

"O.K., baby, O.K. but ..."

103

"Play it."

"Can I finish my drink?"

"Sure."

After a while I walked over to the two dollar window.

"Number six," I said, "once."

It was my last two dollars.

Number six paid $23.40.

I watched my horse go down into the Winner's Circle like I do all my winners, and I felt as proud of him as if I had ridden him or raised him. I felt like cheering and telling everybody he was the greatest horse that had ever lived, and I felt like reaching out and hugging him around the neck, even though I was two or three hundred feet away.

Instead I lit my cigarette and pretended I was bored.

Then I headed back to the bar, kind of to see how she took it, intending to stay pretty far away. But they weren't there.

I ordered a double backed by a beer, drank both, ordered up again and drank at my leisure, studying the next race. When the 5 minute warning blew, they still hadn't shown up and I went off to place my bet.

I blew it. I blew them all. And the woman and her boyfriend never showed. At the end of the last race I had 35 cents, a 1958 Ford, about two gallons of gas and one night's rent left.

I went into the men's room and stared in the mirror at my face in disgust. I *looked* like I knew something, but it was a lie, I was a fake and there's nothing worse in the world than when a man suddenly realizes and admits to himself that he's a phoney, after spending all his time up to then trying to convince himself that he wasn't. I stared at all the sinks and pipes and bowls and I felt like them, worse than them: I'd rather be them.

I swung out the door and stood there feeling like a hare or a tortoise or somebody needing a good bath, and then I felt her pressing against me like the good part of myself suddenly coming back with a rush. I noticed how green her dress was, and I didn't care what happened next: seeing her again had made it O.K.

"Where've you been?" she asked hurriedly. "I've been looking all over for you!"

What the hell is this? I started to say, you've been looking for me?

"Here comes *Tommy!*" She hesitated, and I felt her push something into my hand. Then she walked out, carefully, slowly to meet him. I jammed whatever it was into my pocket and walked out to the parking lot. I got into my car, lit my next-to-last cigarette, leaned back and dropped my hand into my pocket.

I unfolded 5 one hundred dollar bills, one fifty, 2 tens and a five. "Your half," the note said, "with thanks. Nicki." And then I saw the phone number.

I sat there and watched all the cars leave; I sat there and watched the sun completely disappear; I sat there and watched a man change a flat tire; and then I drove out of there slowly, like an old man, letting it hit me, little by little, and scared to death I'd run somebody over or be unable to stop for a red light. Then I thought about the nickel I'd thrown away and I started to laugh like crazy. I laughed so hard I had to park the car. And when the guy who'd changed his flat passed me and I saw his white blob of a face staring back I had to laugh all over again. I even honked my horn and hollered at him.

Poor devil: he had no soul.

nature poem

you are 50,000 Light Years
running through my brain in
tracksuits or
you are like sitting in a bar
with enough money
with a good drink
and looking through the window
at the snow

you are the dead fish of miracle
moving

you are the love-god of ice cream
phantasy
you have diminished the screaming of
children as they drink my
blood
I think that you have killed landlords
wanting rent
and also bad
tigers

there is a white flower laying against
my screen
like a whore
like a cat
like a white flower

I could not go to work
tonight because I could not

stop living
and now I am lying in bed
looking at the white flower.

warning

upon your darkened red mouth wild birds scream
and bowls of fish swim their jungles,
a China morning, a withered noon of axes and
witches;
you desire a man-plagued sun and strands of
fiber calling my name;
beware, I am not your silly husband,
I am your silly lover
and of all your silly lovers,
the last one here.

answer to a note on the dresser:

the price of the sun is the tulip rotting black
and the prince on his knees
and a boy born without eyes
and a kitten without a bird,
                    nothing but twine
and waiting
          and whores dipping hearts in poison,
and exhaust and exhaustion
and the bliss and the kiss of syphilis,
drag down the vines
the broken-foot bottles,
                    I keep saying
ha ha ha the giants
the giant sun
am I, the giant. our sun
tonight
          without sun
your shoes alone without you in them
and I alone frying steaks and drinking beer
and listening to Wagner
the price of the sun,
the price of the sun,
and I don't give a damn if you never come back.

you don't know

you don't know how good it
can get
being in a strange city,
nobody knowing who you
are,
coming in from the low-
paying
job,
forgetting dinner,
taking off your shoes,
climbing onto the bed,
lights out
in that cheap dark
room
living with the roaches
or the mice,
hearing the crackling of
the wallpaper
or the rush of small
feet darting
across the floor.

lifting the wine bottle
there in the moonlight
or in the light of the
street lamps and the
neon signs,
the wine entering your
body,
the flare of your match
lighting a

cigarette.

you don't know how good
it can get
without women,
without a telephone,
without a tv set,
without a car.

with the bathroom down
the hall.

relaxed in the dark
hearing the voices of the
other roomers,
hearing pans rattling,
food frying,
toilets flushing,
arguments,
occasional
laughter.

you don't know
the names of the
streets,
who the mayor is
or how long you
will remain.

you will remain
until the next city,
the next room,
the next low-paying
job.

the mice will become

bolder.
one will come up on
the dresser,
climb up on the handle
of the coffee cup,
hang there,
looking at you.

you will get up and
approach the mouse.
you are the
intruder.
as you get closer
he still will not
move.
his eyes and your eyes
will intermix.
it is the clash of
centuries.

then he will leap
through the air
in the darkness and
be gone.

you will return to
the bed, smiling,
thinking, he's lucky,
he doesn't have to
pay the rent.

you will drink some more
from the wine
bottle,
then rise, take off your
clothing, stack it on

the chair.
you will sit up against
the pillow,
listening to the cars
passing below.

you will get up,
check the alarm clock,
see that it is set for
7:30 a.m.

then, foolishly, you'll
have to put your pants
on again
to make a bathroom
run.

the hall will be quiet
and empty,
the lights will be out,
there will only be
darkness under each
doorway.
the roomers are
sleeping.

your face
in the bathroom mirror
will grin at
you.

then you will walk
back to your room,
get the pants off
again, hang them over
the back of the

chair that is possibly
older than
you.

the last drink is
best, the last flare of
the match
lighting the last
cigarette.
you hold the match,
still burning,
up against the palm
of your right
hand.

long life line.

too bad.

then to stretch out,
the covers up
against your
neck.
warm covers.
rented covers.
covers of love.

the day seeps slowly
back through your
consciousness.
not much.

then, like the other
roomers, you are
asleep.
you are equal to the

side of a
triangle,
to a mountain in
Peru,
to a tiger
licking its
paw.

you don't know
how good it can be
until you've been
there.

let not

let not the people be your
foundation,
not the young girls,
not the old girls,
not the young men,
not the old men,
not those in-between,
not any of these,
let not the people be your
foundation.

rather
build on sand
build on landfills,
build over cesspools,
build over graveyards,
build even over water,
but don't build on the
people.

they are a bad bet,
the worst bet you can make.

build it elsewhere,
anywhere else,
anywhere
but on the people,
the headless, heartless
mass
mucking up the
centuries,

the days,
the nights,
the towns, the cities, the
nations,
the earth,
the stratosphere,
mucking up the
light,
mucking up
all chance,
here,
totally mucking
it up
then
now
tomorrow.

anything,
compared to the people,
is a foundation worth
searching for.

anything.

the death of a roach

... when the last fig falls and we are pruned from light,
our golden ladies gleaned of love—
                              infest us with the mercy
of stone.

calisthenic tempest, kingly pain
the flowers held kisses and blossoms
crackling with lightning power against our
pinioned brain; I watch the roach
as prophets of exile drink
and break their cups.

the grasses held long and green their secrets.

now, old ladies cassocked like monks
treadmill the slow poor stairs
bumping their angry canes: solatium! solatium!
and they close themselves in shawls
as the sun rallies new buds to color,
and they think ... of onions and biscuits
(beautiful day, isn't it?)
(did you hear Father Francis? Sunday?)

the roach climbs
(the mirrors of love are broken)
blind yet begotten with life, a dedicated wraith
of pus and antennae.

I take him from his task
with a stab of a finger that wretches
like a stomach against the sick black twisted

death; no bandores here, or philosophical canvas to color
                                        with tantamounts.

I hide him in some hasty packet and flush his ugliness away,
and above me in the mirror, consumed and listening there:
a crevice, a demon declaring his hand:—

all about me the old ladies cackle enraged, infirm
                                        and bleeding
violate,
        lepisma,
                they attack my tired guts with canes and pins,
                with scrolls and bibles, with celebrations of
                witchcraft
they maim my brain with mercy until I fall witless and ill,
shouting
                shouting roominghouses and grass,
                shouting apes and horses,
                shouting
                        flowers and kisses: the insects are suspect—
man can only destroy himself.

it's been months now: the most
horrible thing I have ever
felt.
and I might have avoided
it.
might have.
maybe not.
but I didn't and in a way I
couldn't.
it occurred more quickly than
I could respond.
I should have been more
able,
more ready.

and for some
what was a horror for me
might have been
trivial to them.
but I have never been
"them."

it's over now.
the pain of that should be
finished.
but it stays with me.
and that I did not act in
time to prevent it—
but that moment is
gone.
and

I truly hate myself
for the first
time.

I will never recover.
it comes back to me
again and
again.

and in its aftermath,
nothing will ever be
quite right
again—
walking down a
hill,
getting out of
bed,
common tasks,
celebrations,
just
happenings
are
reshaped
by that occurrence.

*I was gored
by my own
stupidity.*

it was an animal.
it was an animal,
caused by some
human
thing?

would that it *was*
human.

so I could have
considered it
trivial.

right now

the party's over, the rooster is
crowing and they've called in
the dice, the dancing girls are
snoring, the mice are crawling
in the paper cups, the donkey is
pinned to the tail, the fable has
crawled away to die, love is
covered with dust, the temples
are empty, the bird has flown
the cage, the cage encloses a
midget heart weeping, the dream
has taken a dive and I sit
looking at my hands, looking at
my hands
empty of the sound of the
moment.

the sheep

in centuries past
audiences at symphony concerts
were not afraid to act out their
displeasure at works which
offended
them.

in our time
I have either attended or
listened to
hundreds of concerts
and never have I heard an
audience
express even the mildest displeasure
with any
work.

have our musical artists improved
to such an
extent?

or is it the decay of courage,
the inability of the
mass mind to
reach its own
decisions?

not only in the world of
music
but in the other
world?

124

the next time you hear
a symphony concert
note
the obedient applause,
the death of the bluebird,
the shading of the sun;
the hooves of the horses from
hell
pounding on the barren
ground
of the human
spirit.

piss

remember once I was sitting in this hotel
room when my woman came in drunk and said,
"Christ, I couldn't hold it, I had to piss in the
elevator!"
I was drunk too, I was barefoot and in
my shorts.
I got up and walked out the door and down
the hall and pushed the elevator
button.
it came up.
the door opened.
the elevator was empty but sure enough
there in the corner was the
puddle.
as I was standing there a man and a
woman came out of their place
and walked toward the
elevator.
the door was beginning to close
so I held it open with my hand
so they could get
on.
as the door began to close I heard the
woman say,
"that man was in his shorts."
and just as it closed I heard the man say,
"and he pissed in the elevator."

I went back to the room and told her,
"they think I pissed in the elevator."

"who?" she asked.

"people."

"what people?"

"the people who saw me standing
in my shorts."

"well, screw them," she said.

she was sitting there drinking a glass
of wine.

"take a bath," I said.

"you take a bath," she said.

"at least take a shower," I said.

"you take a shower," she said.

I sat down and poured a glass of
wine.

we were always arguing about
something.

last fight

he's just a handler
now.
he's in the gym
watching the young
boxers spar.
he knows all the
moves,
watches the foot-
work, the counter-
punching, the leads,
the hooks, the
timing, the
will.

he was a fighter
once,
went a number of
ten rounders.

now he watches
the action,
squinting,
analyzing.

he's got a gut
now
it bulges out
under his old
sweat shirt.

it's an afternoon

in the gym.
he can hear them
grunt,
he can hear the
shots, the
big gloves
landing.

inside his head
he can see
himself in the
ring,
he can hear the
screams of the
young girls
again,
the yelling of
the men,
he can feel the
lights,
the canvas
under his feet,
the ropes
squaring him
into
battle.

son-of-a-bitch,
what a
time,
son-of-a-bitch,
what a
life!

then he returns
to reality.

son-of-a-bitch,
he's old.
he's got a bucket
and a
towel.
well, it beats
sucking buttermilk
through a
straw.

the rounds are
finished,
something else
now waits.

yeah.

there'll be
no more split
decisions for
that
son-of-a-
bitch.

defining the magic

a good poem is like a cold beer
when you need it,
a good poem is a hot turkey
sandwich when you're
hungry,
a good poem is a gun when
the mob corners you,
a good poem is something that
allows you to walk through the streets of
death,
a good poem can make death melt like
hot butter,
a good poem can frame agony and
hang it on a wall,
a good poem can let your feet touch
China,
a good poem can make a broken mind
fly,
a good poem can let you shake hands
with Mozart,
a good poem can let you shoot craps
with the devil
and win,
a good poem can do almost anything,
and most important
a good poem knows when to
stop.

often it is the only
thing
between you and
impossibility.
no drink,
no woman's love,
no wealth
can
match it.

nothing can save
you
except
writing.

it keeps the walls
from
falling.
the hordes from
closing
in.

it blasts the
darkness.

writing is the
ultimate
psychiatrist,
the kindliest
god of all the
gods.

writing stalks
death.
it knows no
quit.

and writing
laughs
at itself,
at pain.

it is the last
expectation,
the last
explanation.

that's
what it
is.

my friend says, how can you write so many poems
from that window? I write from the womb,
he tells me. the dark thing of pain,
the featherpoint of pain ...

well, this is very impressive
only I know that we both receive a good many
rejections, smoke a great many cigarettes,
drink too much and attempt to steal each other's
women, which is not poetry at all.

and he reads me his poems
he always reads me his poems
and I listen and do not say too much,
I look out of the window,
and there is the same street
my street
my drunken, rained-on, sunned-on,
childrened-on street,
and at night I watch this street
sometimes
when it thinks I am not looking,
the one or 2 cars moving quietly,
the same old man, still alive, on his
nightly walk,
the shades of houses down,
love has failed but
hangs on
then lets go
as the tomcats chase it,
but now it is daylight and children

who will some day be old men and women
walking through last moments,
these children run around a red car
screaming their good nothings,
then my friend puts down his poem ...

well, what do you think? he asks.

try so and so, I name a magazine,
and then oddly
I think of guitars under the sea
trying to play music;
it is sad and good and quiet.
he sees me at the window.
what's out there?

look, I say,
and see ...

he is eleven years younger than I.
he turns from the window: I need a beer,
I'm out of beer.

I walk to the refrigerator
and the subject is closed.

the strong man

I went to see him, there in that place in
Echo Park
after my shift at the
post office.
he was a huge bearded fellow
and he sat in his chair like a
Buddha
and he was my Buddha, my guru,
my hero, my roar of
light.
sometimes he wasn't kind
but he was always more than
interesting.
to come from the post office
a slave
to that explosion of light
confounded me,
but it was a remarkable and
delightful
confusion.

thousands of books upon
hundreds of subjects
lay rotting in his
cellar.

to play chess with him was
to be laughed off the
board.
to challenge him
physically or

mentally was
useless.

but he had the ability to
listen to your
persiflage
patiently
and then the ability
to sum up its
weaknesses,
its delusions in
one sentence.

I often wondered how
he put up with my
railings; he was kind,
after all.

the nights lasted 7,
8 hours.
I had myself.
he had himself
and a beautiful woman
who quietly smiled as she
listened to
us.
she worked at a drawing
board,
designing things.
I never asked what and
she never
said.

the walls and the ceilings
were pasted over
with hundreds of odd

legends,
like the last words of
a man in an electric
chair,
or gangsters on their
death beds,
or a murderer's instructions
to her children;
photos of Hitler, Al Capone,
Chief Sitting Bull,
Lucky Luciano.
it was an endless honey-
comb of strange faces
and
utterances.

it was darkly refreshing.

and at odd rare times
even I was interesting.

then the Buddha would
nod.

he recorded everything on
tape.

sometimes on another
night he would play a
tape back for
me.
and then I would
realize how pitiful, how
cheap, how
inept I sounded.

he seldom did.

at times I wondered why
the world had not
discovered
him.
he made no effort to be
discovered.

he had other
visitors,
always wild, original
refreshing
folk.

it was crazier than the
sun burning up the
sea,
it was the bats of hell
whirling about the
room.

that was decades ago
and he is still
alive.

he made a place when
there was no
place.
a place to go when all
was closing in,
strangling, crushing,
debilitating,
when there was no
voice, no sound,
no sense,

he lent his easy
saving
natural
grace.

I feel that I owe him
one,
I feel that I owe him
many.

but I can hear him
now, that same
voice
as when he sat
so huge
in that same
chair:

"Nothing is owed,
Bukowski."

you're finally wrong,
this time,
John Thomas, you
bastard.

the terror

the terror is in viewing the human
face
and then hearing it talk
and watching the creature
move.
the terror is in knowing its
motives.
the terror is in seeing it
skinned,
opened
for the internal view of the
spirit.
the terror is looking at the
eyes.
the terror is knowing of the
centuries of its
doings.
the terror is the unchangeability
of it.
and its multiplicity,
its duplicity, it's
everywhere, a giant mass
of it
self-revered,
self-serving,
self-destructive,
the terror of no selves
spreading from here and now into
space,
cluttering the universe,
marring pure space,

poisoning hope,
raping chance,
going on,
this massive zero of
life
labeled
Humanity.
the terror, the
horror,
the waste of them
and you and
me
through and
through.

the kiss-off

it was one of those
half-ass
literary gatherings
and this girl dropped to her
knees on the rug and
said to
him:
"O, Mr. C., let me kiss
that thumb
that great amputated thumb
that appeared in that great American novel
On the Road!"

Mr. C. held out the amputated thumb
and she kissed
it
and we all came
all around all
around, we all came all
around.

Jimmy Foxx died an alcoholic
in a skidrow hotel
room.
Beau Jack ended up shining
shoes,
just where he
began.
there are dozens, hundreds
more, maybe
thousands more.
being an athlete grown old
is one of the cruelest of
fates,
to be replaced by others,
to no longer hear the
cheers and the
plaudits,
to no longer be
recognized,
just to be an old man
like other old
men.

to almost not believe it
yourself,
to check the scrapbook
with the yellowing
pages.
there you are,
smiling;
there you are,

victorious;
there you are,
young.

the crowd has other
heroes.
the crowd never
dies,
never grows
old
but the crowd often
forgets.

now the telephone
doesn't ring,
the young girls are
gone,
the party is
over.

this is why I chose
to be a
writer.
if you're worth just
half-a-damn
you can keep your
hustle going
until the last minute
of the last
day.
you can keep
getting better instead
of worse,
you can still keep
hitting them over the
wall.

through darkness, war,
good and bad
luck
you keep it going,
hitting them out,
the flashing lightning
of the
word,
beating life at life,
and death too late to
truly win
against
you.

THE UNACCOMMODATING UNIVERSE

Carl sat at the end of the bar where he wouldn't have to deal with anybody. He kept his head down and didn't look at anybody. He was on his second drink, a vodka-7. Then he heard two girls behind him talking. He hadn't heard them walk in.

"Well, we can't sit at the bar," one said, "no two empty stools together."

"Maybe we can get a table?"

"No, the tables are full ..."

"Shit."

"Well, let's go someplace else."

"No, this is where the action is!"

Carl felt a finger explore under and around his collar. Then he felt it tickle his ear. One of the girls giggled. Carl didn't move. Then he said, without looking around, "Didn't we know each other in Toledo?"

"Athens, Georgia," came the answer. The finger withdrew.

"I'm Toni," one of the girls said.

"I'm Cristina," said the other girl.

"I'm Carl," said Carl, still not looking around.

"Could you move down one stool?" said Toni. "We can't find a place to sit together."

"Too fucking bad," said Carl.

He drained his drink and nodded Blinky the Barkeep in for a refill.

"Blinky," said Carl, "I need a ticket to the Laker's game."

"When?"

"Tonight."

"I'll see what I can do." Blinky walked off.

Toni leaned against Carl, pressing her breasts against his back.

"Tell us something about yourself," she said.

"I've got AIDS."

"Bullshit!"

Toni pulled away.

"Hey, we don't have to fuck around with this asshole! There are plenty of NICE men around here!"

"Yeah, he's an *asshole*!" Cristina said.

The girls walked down to the other end of the bar. They were in their mid-twenties, well-dressed. Toni was the redhead, Cristina was the blonde. They had nice buttocks, were slim-hipped, long of leg. They had bright healthy eyes, clever smiles. They were … attractive.

They stood behind Barney the Hump, talking to him.

Then the phone rang. Blinky answered it and then brought the phone down and placed it in front of Carl. Carl picked it up.

"Hello?"

It was Rissy. Rissy was crying.

"I gotta see ya, Jesus, I gotta see ya!"

"Rissy, there is nobody you got to see unless it's a shrink."

"The son-of-a-bitch beat me, Carl! I'm all bruises and lumps, I can't go out on the street!"

"Good. You need a rest."

Carl hung up. He went for his drink. The phone rang again. Carl winked at Blinky and picked it up.

"Lion's Nuts Bar."

She was still crying. "I gotta see ya, don't ya understand? Don't ya have no compassion?"

"Our marriage has been annulled. I like the sound of that word: ANNULLED."

He hung up.

There was a scream down at the end of the bar. It was Toni. Then Carl saw the girls moving briskly back toward him and the exit. They stopped at his stool. Toni stood in front and Cristina stood behind her as they faced Carl.

Toni was in a fury. "THAT SON-OF-A-BITCH SLAPPED ME! NO SON-OF-A-BITCH SLAPS ME! NO SON-OF-A-BITCH SLAPS TONI EBERT! NOBODY! NOBODY! I NEVER SEEN A BAR SO FULL OF ASSHOLES! YOU GUYS FAGS? ARE YOU AFRAID OF WOMEN? OR ARE YA FUCKIN' STUPID?"

"We're just fuckin' stupid," somebody said.

"YOU CAN SURE AS SHIT SAY THAT AGAIN!"

"We're just fuckin' stupid," somebody said again.

Blinky walked down to the end of the bar.

"Girls, I'm sorry ..."

"SORRY AIN'T ENOUGH, ASSHOLE. I'M GOING TO HAVE THIS DUMP TRASHED!"

"I thought it already was," said Blinky.

"YOU PRICK!"

The girls turned on their heels and were gone into the night.

Blinky walked up to Carl. He slid the Laker's ticket at him.

Carl reached for his wallet. Blinky waved him off and walked down to Barney the Hump.

"Why'd you slap that girl, Barney?"

"WHY? HEY, WHY, HUH? WHY, HUH?"

"Yeah, why?"

"That whore stuck her finger in my ear!"

"What's the matter? You got a problem with that?"

"I just don't like girls who jerk me around," Barney said with a grin.

The phone rang again. Carl picked it up.

"Lion's Nuts ..."

"I'll kill myself, that's what I'll do, I'LL KILL MYSELF!"

"No chance," said Carl and hung up.

The hardest thing about life, he thought, was dealing with other people's problems. You could be consumed with other people's problems: they were always having car crashes or going mad or forgetting to pay the rent, or they left the butter out, fucked strangers, had insomnia, or—if they slept —had unhappy dreams. And they never considered the fact that you had your own miseries to unravel. Ah, well ...

Carl nodded Blinky in for another refill.

"You gonna make the game?" Blinky asked.

"Sure. I always arrive late to beat the traffic and leave early to beat the traffic."

"Why go at all?"

"What do you want me to do? Sit around and listen to Chopin?"

"Carl, those two girls were fine looking. How come you passed?"

"I don't know. Fucking to me is like shaving. I guess it's something I have to do now and then but I feel like putting it off."

"You getting old?"

"Maybe just wise. You know, fucking is nature's idea."

"A good idea, I think."

"Yeah, but overrated."

"You're putting me on ..."

Blinky moved off ...

It was maybe ten minutes later that the girls came back. They stood just inside the door. And in front of them stood their pimp. Big and dark. But he was different than most. He wasn't one of those slick pimps. He wasn't dressed to shine. He had on an old overcoat and heavy workman's shoes. He was very big with a razor scar curling down the left side of his face. He looked like a good natured guy who could get very mean and he looked ready to get very mean.

"Gentlemen, I hear my girls have been having some trouble in here."

Nobody answered.

"It makes me unhappy when somebody makes one of my girls unhappy. And I don't like them or me to be unhappy."

150

Blinky moved forward a bit, then stopped.

"Listen, man, it was just a mistake. One of those things, you know."

"No, I don't know."

The pimp just stood there.

He stood there and stood there. It was very quiet. The girls waited behind the big guy. It was an agony of tension. Every small sound could be heard. The dripping of the bar faucet, the slight hum of the electric clock and the almost soothing sound of the street traffic.

Then Mickey the Bookie, the drunkest of them all, sitting at bar center said, "Yeah. So shit. What ya gonna do?"

The pimp moved at once. He moved in behind Mickey before Mickey could react. Mickey was working on a draft beer. His glass was half full. The pimp took the glass and spilled the contents on the bar.

"What I'm going to do, I'm going to do. But the first thing YOU'RE going to do is lap that up!"

"Kiss my ass," Mickey said.

Mickey had on a blue Dodger's baseball cap. The pimp flipped it off, grabbed Mickey by the hair and then he had the razor at his throat.

"Get it! Lap it up! Every last motherfucking drop! NOW!"

He pushed Mickey's head down and Mickey's tongue came out. He began lapping at the bar.

"Hey, man," said Blinky, "you ..."

"SHUT UP!"

The pimp held Mickey's head down and Mickey's tongue worked up the beer. Then he let him go. He stepped back. Mickey straightened up and lit a cigarette. The cigarette trembled in his mouth. He inhaled, then exhaled a pitiful curl of smoke.

"You guys," said the pimp, "got to learn that my ladies are real ladies and must be treated accordingly. They offer a service that keeps mankind contented and I don't want them pushed around."

Carl turned on his stool.

"All right, whatever we did, it's done. Maybe it was wrong. It probably was. We're sorry for that. But you're making too much of it."

"I'll decide what's too much," the pimp said. "I intend to see that this kind of shit doesn't continue."

"So what are you going to do?" asked Carl, looking at the razor in his hand. "Kill somebody? You want somebody's balls in a sack?"

"I wouldn't mind that, I might arrange that."

"Come on, Jason," said Toni, "let's get out of here. We don't need any more. We don't need this shit."

The pimp nodded her off.

"I want to know which guy hit my woman. Now, whoever hit my woman, I want him to speak up."

There was silence.

"You might as well speak up. All I gotta do is ask my woman."

There was more silence. Barney the Hump drained his drink and stood up.

"I hit your whore. She stuck her finger in my ear and messed with me and if she did the same thing again I'd hit her again."

"Mister," said the big pimp, "it's evident your mother never taught you manners."

The pimp moved forward. Barney the Hump squared off in front of the crapper. Barney missed with a right as the pimp came in and they both crashed through the crapper door. It splintered like balsa wood. There was a scramble in the crapper and the pimp came out holding Barney in a death grip. He spun him once, then lifted him and threw him across the bar and into the bar mirror. The mirror shattered, bottles fell and smashed as Barney fell behind the bar and lay motionless, face down. Then a full quart of gin came sailing from somewhere and caught the pimp behind the ear. He staggered a moment, then righted himself.

152

Then he roared, "I'LL GET ALL YOU MOTHER-
FUCKERS!"

Patrons were running out the front and out the back.
The big pimp had his razor out and he sliced through the
motion, sliced part of an ear from Mickey the Bookie.
Suddenly the lights went out. The girls screamed, ran. There
was the flash of a gunshot and the pimp dropped his razor
and grabbed his belly.

"Christ, you chickenshit ..."

Carl ran out the back way and into the alley and then
out of there and west down 6th Street. People were just
strolling along and he slowed to a fast walk. He circled the
corner and went down to where his car was parked. He got
in, kicked it over, looking back at the bar. Nobody was com-
ing out of there. Then the pimp walked out. He looked pow-
erful in the early night. He stood there a moment like a man
looking for a cab. Then he fell forward not able to put out his
hands to break the fall. His head hit first, bounced, then he
was still. Carl drove off to the sound of an approaching siren.

Carl unlocked the door, put the chain on and flicked on the
light. Rissy was sitting on the couch. There was a half-a-fifth
of scotch on the table and Rissy was drunk, hair down in her
face. She was smoking a king-sized cigarette, a red glow on
the end of it. She coughed.

"Hey, where ya been, lover boy? Out fuckin'?"

"Christ, what are you doing here?"

"I wanna talk. I told you he hit me! I wanna talk!"

Carl sat down, took a hit straight from the bottle.

"There's nothing to talk about."

"Hey, that's been our PROBLEM, lover boy! We never
talked about things!"

"We don't have any problem. Our marriage is annulled."

Carl sat to her left. She reached out a hand, touched
him, and as she did so she spilled some of her drink in her
lap. The long glowing cigarette was in her mouth and she
smiled around it.

153

"Hey, what do you think? I'm NEVER going to let you go! It's love! True love!"

"Ah, shit," said Carl. He lifted the fifth and had another hit.

Rissy put her cigarette out in the ashtray, tossed off her drink, filled it again, lit another cigarette.

"That son-of-a-bitch beat me up, can you imagine? That son-of-a-bitch BEAT me!"

"What did you do? Were you screwing around?"

She looked at him, hair still down in her face. Her speech was slurred. She sat with her cigarette in one hand, her drink in the other:

"What's THAT got to do with it? You don't BEAT people! People have their rights! Don't ya think?"

Carl didn't answer. He picked up a cigarette and the lighter. He bent over the lighter, flicked it. The flame was too full. As he lit the cigarette he burned his nose.

"God damn it," he said.

Rissy reached out and touched him again.

"Whatsa matter, honey?"

Then she picked up the remote control, switched on the tv set and they both sat waiting for the screen to come to life.

who said, "you've kept me going for two
years, it's really amazing to meet you."

"thank you," I answered, "but who's
going to keep me going?"

I've asked this question before and
all I ever get back is a gentle
smile.

but it's a good question.

they have no notion that I may consider
suicide several times a
week.

they've read some of my books
and that's enough for
them.

but I only write that stuff,
I can't read
it.

the sun was rather diminished,
the dog came in low,
11:32 a.m.
Wednesday in the year of
our Lord,
all the man heard was the
low gurgling growl,
then the beast had ripped
his thigh,
it was summertime,
the scream parted the
air,
the beast
pirouetted,
leaped powerfully,
sailed toward the
man's
throat,
flowers grew in the
flower beds,
the lawn was newly
mowed,
the man threw up
his hands
against the bared
fangs,
shrank away,
the beast bounced
off,
landed on all
fours,

the small finger
of the man's
right hand
in his
mouth.

the dog stood
dumbly,
then dropped the
finger.

it was a majestic
and beautiful
animal.

its fur rose
along its back
and about the
neck.

it began circling
the man
rapidly.

"JESUS CHRIST!
JESUS CHRIST,
HELP ME!"

two men came
running from the neighboring
back yard.
one was fat and
bald
with a face like
an owl.
the other was

thin with a very
white face
with a large
birthmark,
purple-black,
shaped like a
walnut.

"BRIGGS!" they
yelled,
"BRIGGS!
STOP THAT!"

Briggs paused, then
trotted off into the
back yard.

the man held his
hand
up against his
chest
and covered it
with his
other hand.

the man was
sobbing, sobbing
choking
sobs.

"I'll KILL that
fucking dog!
I'll KILL both
of you!
what's the matter?
are you CRAZY?

ARE YOU
CRAZY?"

then the fat man
with the face
like an
owl
saw something
on the
lawn.

he walked over
and looked down
at it.

it was the
finger.

"what's this?"
he asked.
"what's this?"

an old man on a
bicycle rode past
on the sidewalk
he was in red
and white shorts,
wore goggles
and a yellow
helmet.
on the back of
his sweat shirt
it said,
MEAT ME,
BABY.

he rode on
by.

it was 11:39 a.m.
in the year of our
Lord.

the kid

had trouble hitting left
handers so I got him to
switch hit,
then I shifted him from
left to center,
dropped him from
lead-off to the 6th
spot,
also had him work
on the bunt.
I had long talks with
him about his
career,
told him that
concentration was
essential.
I worked hard with
the kid,
had him take
extra batting
practice,
had him switch
to a lighter
bat,
work on
contact,
the power would
come by
itself.
I had him stand
closer to the

plate,
be more
selective at
what he
swung
at.
I worked hard
with the
kid,
played him
every day
but his average
dipped to
.229 and I had
to ship him
to the
minors.

all that talent
and he couldn't get
it
together.
he acted confused,
disoriented.
my guess was
it's some
broad.

poor bastard.
all that
natural talent
shot to
shit.

I've seen it
happen so many

times.

well, I've got
Sunderson out
there now.
he's hitting
.289,
lots of line
drives,
he's adequate
in the
field,
steady.

we oughta be
right in the
race,
come
September.

there were two policemen on motorcycles.
there was a policelady and a policeman
from a squad car.
the car was angled crosswise in the
driveway to the parking lot
of the cafe.

one policeman was calling in
downtown.

there was a man about
23.
he was facing the wall of a
building.
he was obviously an
indigent.
his clothes were greasy and
ill-fitting.
and he had shit his
pants.
the stain was showing
through the back.
he was not cuffed
and he was not directly
facing the
wall.
he was turned a little to
one side,
peeking at his
captors.
the police seemed to be

hardly
watching him.
they were
indifferent,
talking among
themselves.

it was a beautiful winter
afternoon.

I walked past the scene
on the way to the
cafe.

as I did, the lady policeman
gave me a hateful look
that said, buzz off, this is
none of your
business.

it was and it
wasn't.

I went into the cafe and had
lunch.
when I came out
everybody was
gone
and it was still a
beautiful winter
afternoon.

poor bastard had shit his
pants.

my car hadn't been

stolen.
I got in and drove
off.

bad day

the jellyfish has a purpose,
the hyena,
the tick,
the rat,
the roach
each filled with their
swollen
light.

my light is
out.
who did this to
me?

the dick

I was sitting in my office in the dark
not thinking about much, well, maybe a little about
the Barker caper
when the door opened real slow—
I was not expecting any visitors—
I slid my hand slowly into my pocket and fondled
my 45.

hell, it's a dame, a looker, dressed to kill, she's rocking
there on her high heels and long legs, one garter belt
showing through her slitted dress. She said, lighting a
cigarette, "remember me?"

"well, no," I said. "I've got a metal plate in my head and
I drink too much vodka."

"cut the crap," she hissed like a tigress, "we made love 7 times
the night before last!"

"you cut the crap," I told her. "I haven't had it up since
        Gettysburg."

I saw her reach into her purse, I saw the glint of metal in the
        moonlight
coming through the dirty Venetian blinds.
I tossed the vodka bottle at her head quicker than you can say
better to cheat on your wife than on your income tax.

I got up, walked around, bent over the vodka bottle, it was all
        right,
no breakage.

168

then I looked at her, out, cold and beautiful.
I began to get ideas.
I lifted her dress.
but then she opened her eyes.

"you killed Eddie," she said.

"who?" I asked.

"Eddie Blankenship."

"wait," I told her, "I'm Eddie Blankenship."

"Christ," she said.

"No, not him. Eddie Blankenship."

I went around behind the desk, uncapped the vodka and had a
good hit.
the whole thing didn't make sense.

she sat in a chair, crossing her legs high.

"I'll solve the case for you," I told her, "but I don't come
    cheap."

"money's no object," she said, her pure gold earrings
    shining in
the moonlight coming through the dirty Venetian blinds. "I'm
    Marcy Peats
Booty the 3rd, I've got billions."

"20 bucks," I said.

"you're on."

she threw back her beautiful head and laughed.
I fondled my gun under the desk.

"well, it's like this," I told her. "I couldn't have killed Eddie
Blankenship because I'm him."
I paused.

"so!" she smiled a smile that would melt a steel
gate.

"so," I said, "there have to be TWO Eddie Blankenships."

"sounds like crap to me," she said.

"baby," I said, "crap don't sound. I'm giving you the
        frigging facts."

just then the door swung open and here stood this ragged
        looking guy,

no class, not much ass, not much of anything.

"I'm Eddie Blankenship," he said.

"well, suck a rabbit's tits," I said.

"hello, Eddie," the doll said to him.

"hi, baby," he said, "what's this punk doing sitting behind
        my desk?"

"your desk and what Army's desk?" I snarled.

"me and the Canadian Royal Mounties!" he snarled.

"that's no Army!" I yelled.

170

"your mother's armpits!" he screamed.

he reached.

I reached.

two bright roaring flashes.

his bullet bounced off my steel plate.
he crumpled.

I went around, bent over him, took his wallet, then felt his
pulse.

I looked up at her.

"this man is dead," I told her.

"you killed Eddie Blankenship!" she screamed.

I saw her reach into her purse.
there was another bright roaring flash.
she pitched forward off her chair.

I bent over her.
in her right hand was a fingernail file.
I emptied her purse.
I felt her breasts, her legs.
I felt her pulse.
she was dead.

I walked around behind my desk, had a hit of vodka and
sat there.

the moon came in through the dirty Venetian blinds.
I had 2 dead bodies and half-a-bottle of
vodka.

it was time to do some thinking.
I was in some hell of a jam.
I had to do something.
I reached for the phone.
I got the operator.
I asked her to connect me with my mother in
Iowa City.

collect.

then I sat there listening to the phone
ring.

car on its side in the moonlight,
wheels toward the sky still spinning.
a man crawls out of the broken window
of the door.
he is wearing a white shirt splotched
with blood.
inside the car the radio is still playing
loudly.
the man walks across the street, sits down
on
the curbing.
he was on his way to pick up a girlfriend
for dinner.
he will be late, very late.
in fact, there will be no dinner.
the wheels have stopped spinning.
it was just one of those things which
happen
like the fall of the Roman Empire.
somebody puts a blanket around the man.
he asks for a cigarette, gets one.
somebody lights it for him, he inhales,
exhales.
then the ambulance is there.
the police cruiser.
"he ran a red light," said the man to the cop.
"I hit the brakes,
clipped his rear end and somehow flipped.
that son of a bitch."
"he left the scene?" the cop asked.

"yeah," said the man, "the son of a bitch."
the people stood off a little in the distance,
staring.
their night had become interesting.
all of them were glad they weren't the man
sitting on the
curbing.
it was better than tv.
"you been drinking?" asked the cop,
"I smell liquor."
"I had a few beers …"
"how many?"
"2 … 3 …"
it was getting interesting.
the car radio was still playing.
bad rap music.
a boy of about 6 started dancing to
the music.
two ambulance drivers walked up.
one of them needed a shave.
the one who needed a shave asked
the cop,
"can he walk or will he need a stretcher?"
"can you walk to the ambulance?"
the cop asked
the man.
"sure," he said.
he stood up and began walking toward the
ambulance.
he took a misstep, seemed to twist to
the right,
then lost his balance and fell.
he hit the street hard.
his head bounced up once, then fell back.
he was still.
it looked ugly.

the ambulance driver who needed a shave
knelt down over him.
it was a hot July night in a decent
neighborhood.
then the radio in the car stopped.
a few of the people turned and walked off.
they had seen enough.
the others waited
in the brilliant and lovely
moonlight.

people

look at the people: elbows, knees,
earlobes, crotches, feet,
noses, lips, eyes, all the parts
usually clothed, and they are
engaged
in whatever they usually do
which is hardly ever
delightful,
their psyches stuffed with
used matter and propaganda,
advertising propaganda, religious
propaganda, sexual propaganda,
political propaganda, assorted
propagandas, and they
themselves are
dull and vicious.
they are dull because they have been
made dull and they are
vicious because they are
fearful of losing what they have.

the people are the biggest
horror show on earth,
have been for
centuries.

you could be sitting in a
room with one of them
now
or with many of
them.

or you could be one
of them.

every time the phone
rings or there is a knock on
the door
I'm afraid it will be one of
the disgusting,
spiritually destroyed
useless
babbling
ugly
fawning
hateful
humans.

or worse, on picking up the
phone the voice I hear
might be my
own,
or upon opening the
door
I will see myself
standing there,
a remnant of the
wasted centuries,
smiling a
false smile,
having learned well,
having forgotten
what I am here
for.

Ransom

Marty drove up the unpaved lane, parked the car and got out. He walked to the small run-down house, opened the door and walked into the kitchen. The Kid was still tied to the chair. Kell was reading an old copy of *Playboy*. Marty sat down and looked at the Kid across the table. Then he got up, went to the refrigerator and got a beer. He looked at the Kid, "You got a tight old man, Kid, I've heard that rich guys are tight, tighter than a virgin."

Kell put the magazine down, "What happened?"

"What happened? The old bastard said 'no' and hung up. Just like that. He likes his money better than his blood-lines. This is his only son."

"Maybe we ought to ask for less."

"Shit, no. I asked for two million and at two million it stays."

"What are we going to do?" asked Kell.

"We're going to get rough. We're going to cut off one of the Kid's ears and mail it to the old man."

"Suppose he don't pay then?"

"Then we send the other ear."

"Listen, fellows," said the Kid, "I ..."

"You shut up," Marty said.

"Listen," said Kell, "I don't like to go around cutting people's ears off."

"I'll do the cutting."

"Suppose he don't pay after two ears?"

"Then we send his balls."

"Listen," said the Kid, "just ..."

"Shut up! I've got to cut off your goddamned ear tonight. Do you think I *like* doing that sort of thing?"

"Let's not do it, Marty."

178

"We've got to. We don't have any choice. Untie the Kid's hands and give him a beer."

The Kid rubbed his wrists where the rope had bound him. His legs were still tied. He lifted the beer.

"I'm sorry, Kid," said Marty. "I told your old man that we were going to lop off one of your ears if he didn't pay up. Know what he said?"

"No."

"He said, 'Go ahead.' Now you might kind of say we got his blessing."

"Dad never cared much for me."

"We're going to have to shame him into caring. We'll ship him your eyeballs if necessary."

"You two guys are worse than my old man! You're bloody filthy cowards!"

"Maybe so. And your old man's tight with his money. So you're caught in the middle."

"It's hard to believe that there are people as cold as you bastards are!"

"There are. We're just two of them. There's plenty more, *plenty*. All members of the human race."

"Isn't there some other way out?" asked Kell, "I don't want to see the Kid lose his ear."

"Get me and the Kid another beer. You're too soft. How'd you ever get into this business?"

"I don't know, Jesus, I just kind of looked around and I was in it. I started with the numbers racket in Philly and ..."

"All right. That's enough history. One way or the other the Kid's ear goes—tonight."

"You're a chickenshit bastard!" said the Kid.

"Now is that any way to talk to a man who has given you two free beers?"

"Fuck you, you swine!"

"You live in a country whose president was murdered during your lifetime and then whose brother was murdered. You live in a country where people are afraid to walk the streets after dark. Taking one of your ears just about fits the scene."

"It doesn't take any guts to do that."

"Who's talking about guts? If I had any guts I'd be a linebacker for the Chicago Bears. All we want is a little advantage, an edge, something like two million bucks."

Then they were all quiet. Kell got up and got himself a beer. He twisted the cap off and sat down. "This is a nice little place up here in the hills. I'd like to live here instead of always being on the fucking run."

"Yeah. But even with that million in your sock, Kell, you're still going to have to keep running."

"Yeah, but the women will be better."

"Women are all pretty much the same inside. What you call a better woman, well she just has a better facade. It doesn't mean that much."

"I'll take that better facade."

"We're going to have to sterilize a butcher knife."

"How we going to do that?"

"On the stove. Over the flame. We gag the Kid and lop it off. *Zip!* It will be over fast."

"Could he bleed to death?"

"He's not that lucky."

"Do you think we really stand a chance to get that ransom?"

"A damn good chance but we're going to have to make some tough moves. For two million you've got to do a few extra things."

"I still don't like it. It makes me sick to think about it."

"Kell, I'm not as hard as I pretend to be either. Get me another beer."

"Shit, let's not do it."

"The old man is calling our hand. We've got to. We've got no choice."

The Kid bent his head down on the table. He vomited. It was mostly the beer but there were bits of undigested food.

180

"Now, Kid, that wasn't nice. That was really unsanitary. But you're scared so I'll forgive you."

Marty got up and found a dish towel and cleaned the tabletop.

"Tie his hands again. Let's get this fucking thing over with!"

"You pricks," said the Kid, "you chickenshit pricks!"

"And gag him so I don't have to hear that dirty language."

Marty walked to the drawer and found the butcher knife. He walked to the stove and turned a burner on. He held the knife over the flame.

"We can go to South America, Kell. We can live there the rest of our lives. Some of the Nazis went down there after the war and they've never found them. A man can pay for protection just like he pays for pussy." He turned the knife over the flame. "And you're right. I'll take that better facade too. I've been to bed with some real hags."

He took the knife from the flame. The Kid was fully tied and gagged. He walked around behind the Kid so he wouldn't have to look into his eyes. He took the left ear gently between his fingers and pulled it away from the Kid's head. "Hey Kell, hold this son-of-a-bitch still!"

The knife was still pink from the heat. He held it between the ear and the skull. He held it there. Then he threw the knife into a corner of the kitchen, hard. It clattered and bounced, then was still.

"Shit! I can't do it! Come on, let's get the hell out of here!"

Marty walked right out of the kitchen and Kell followed him. They walked through the front room and out the front door and to the car. They got in and Marty backed it out of the drive, took a left on the unpaved lane that led down out of the hills. He looked at Kell. "Got a cigarette?" Kell dug out the pack, pulled out two, lit them both and handed one to Marty.

"Thanks, I'll let the old man know where the Kid is as

soon as we get a few hundred miles away. And don't say a fucking thing to me. I don't want to hear a fucking thing out of you!"

It was 9:30 p.m. It was September. The gas tank read full. Marty turned on the radio. Of all things it was Ray Charles. Marty winced. Kell didn't say a fucking thing.

it's difficult for them

some university profs
find me crude, crass, obvious,
repetitive and pornographic
and I often am,
I sometimes deliberately
am
but this should not concern
them,
they have their friends, their
compatriots, their peers
writing the poesy
which they find
admirable.
but why they rage
against me
in their critical essays
is what I find
strange.
now, I don't like their work
either,
find it pale,
contrived, overworked
and a century behind the
times
but
I don't attack them
critically,
I just stop reading them
and I don't hate them,
I don't care how many books
they publish or who does or

doesn't read
them.
yet, they are very concerned
about my existence
and my large readership,
and almost hysterically
upset
that in some places
I am accepted as an
original writer of some
power.

I tend to ignore this, why
can't they?

if they want their place in
literary history,
fine, they can have
it,
I don't give a damn.

all I want to do is
my work
anyway
I choose to do it,
all I want is the next line
and the line after
that.

what they do and who they
are and what they want
and what they say and what
they write
has no interest for me
and, unfortunately for
them, no interest to most others

living, dying or about to be
born, uh
huh.

think of it, there were fellows like
Kierkegaard and Sartre
who found existence
absurd,
who battled against
anxiety and anguish,
nothingness,
nausea,
and death hanging over them
like a
Damocles sword
while there are other men
now
so empty of concern
that their first thought of the
day is
when are they going to have
lunch?
granted, it could be more
comfortable
to live, say, as a fly, an
ant, a mugwump,
but as a human,
just think,
as a human
to live
thusly,
as millions do
again and again.
of course, hell is other
people,

the waste, the waste,
all flushed away
like
it, like
that.

the garage mechanic
walking toward you
with dead
eyes.

chicken giblets

he's like you, she said, he locks himself in
his basement room and he doesn't want
to see anybody.
I want you to meet him.

I don't want to meet him, I said.

we were driving south down Western.

I want some chicken giblets, she said.

god damn it, I said.

what's the matter? she asked.

I want a drink, I said.

well, I want some chicken giblets,
she said.

I pulled into an all-night drive-in,
opened the door, gave her some
money and she went to the
counter and ordered.

it was 3 in the morning.
she stood there eating her chicken
giblets.

two men walked up.
she started talking to them.

she was smiling.
then they all were laughing.

she had finished eating her
giblets
they kept talking and
laughing.

5 minutes, I thought.
then I looked at my watch.
after 5 minutes I backed my car out of
there and drove off.

I was sitting back in my apartment
having scotch with a beer
chaser when there was a knock
on the door.

I got up and opened it.

it was her.

what the hell happened to you?
she asked.

nothing, I said.

well, pay the cabby, she
said.

there was a cabby standing
behind her.

yeah, he said, pay me.

hey buddy, I said, step closer.

he did.

yeah, he said.

go fuck yourself, I said.

hey, man, he said, I gotta get paid!

I didn't ride in your cab, buddy.

but she's yours, he said.

she's not mine, I said.

whose is she then? he asked.

you take her.

I closed the door.

about ten minutes passed.

there was a knock on the door.
I opened it,
it was her.
she pushed her way in.

gimme a drink, she said.

pour your own, I said.

she did.
she sat in a chair with her drink.

my brother stole my purse,
she said, he took all my
money.

190

he's on drugs, I said.

so am I, she said.

it was another 3:45 a.m. in
east Hollywood
and the black sky came in like a
knife
and if you were alive you were
lucky
and if you were dead
you never knew
it.

the lover

at that apartment in east Hollywood
I was often with the hardest numbers
in town.
I don't speak as a misogynist.
I had other people ask me,
"what the hell are you doing, anyhow?"

they were floozies, killers, blanks.

they had bodies, hair, eyes, legs,
parts
and often it was like
sitting with a shark dressed in a
dress, high heels, smoking, drinking,
swallowing pills.

the nights melted into days and the days
collapsed into nights
as we babbled on, sometimes
bedding down, badly.

because of the drink, the uppers, the
downers, I often imagined
things—say, that this one was the
golden girl of the golden heart and
the golden way of laughter and love
and hope.

in the dim smokey light the long hair
looked better than it was, the legs
more shapely, the conversation not as

bare, not as vicious.

I fooled myself pretty well, I even
got myself to thinking that I loved
one of them, the worst one.

I mean, why the hell be negative?

we drank, drugged, stayed
together through sunset,
sunrise, played Scrabble for 8
or ten hours at a
stretch.

each time I went to piss she
stole the money she needed.
she was a survivor, the
bitch.

after one marathon session
of 52 hours of whatever we
were doing
she said, "let's drive to
Vegas and get married?"

"what?" I asked.

"let's drive to Vegas and
get married before we
change our minds!"

"suppose we get married,
then what?"

"then you can have it any
time you want it," she told

me.

I went in to take a piss
to let her steal the money
she needed.

and when I came out I opened
a new bottle of wine
and spoke no more of the
subject.

she didn't come around as
much after that
but there were others.
about the same.
sometimes there were
more than one.
they'd come in twos.
the word got out that
there was an old sucker
in the back court, free
booze and he wasn't
sexually demanding.
(although at times something
would overtake me and I
would grab a body and throw
in a sweaty horse copulation,
mostly, I guess, to see if
I could still do it.)

and I confused the mailman.
there was an old couch on
the porch and many a morning
as he came by I'd be sitting
there with, say, two of them,
we'd be sitting there,

smoking and
laughing.

one day he found me alone.

"pardon me," he said, "but can
I ask you something?"

"sure."

"well, I don't think you're
rich …"

"no, I'm broke."

"listen," he said, "I've been
in the army, I've been around
the world."

"yeah?"

"and I've never seen a man with
as many women as you have.
there's always a different one,
or a different pair …"

"yeah?"

"how do you do it?
I mean, pardon me, but you're kind
of old and you're not exactly a
Casanova, you know?"

"I could be ugly, even."

he shifted his letters from one hand to the
other.

"I mean, how do you do it?"

"availability," I told him.

"what do you mean?"

"I mean, women like a guy who is always
around."

"uh," he said, then walked off to continue his
rounds.

his praise didn't help me.
what he saw wasn't as good as he thought.
even with them around there were unholy periods
    of
drab senselessness, despair,
and worse.

I walked back into my place.
the phone was ringing.

I hoped that it would be a female
voice.

no win

to live in a jungle
where each face is a face of
horror,
where each voice grates,
where bodies walk
without grace,
where the only communion
is between the dead and
the dead.
to live in a place
where empty faces
and common bodies
win
beauty contests.
to live in a place
where being alone
is always better than being
with someone.
to live a lifetime
with just your
fingernails
more real than
the multitudes,
to roll a 7 in hell
with nothing in the
pot,
that's what this life
is.

THE STAR

He sat in the garden chair watching the birds dig into the freshly watered lawn. He was James Stagler, 81, ex-movie star. He was remembered for his major roles in such epic movies as *Skies Over Bermuda*, *The Brooklyn Kid*, *Son of the Devil*, *A Big Kill*, and *The Ten Count*. Those were his principal films, although he had appeared in hundreds of others and had also starred in a Broadway musical, *Kickin' High*.

"*Lunch!*" He heard the woman's voice, and he rose slowly from his chair, made his way gingerly across the lawn toward the house. James entered from the yard door and walked to the dining room table. He still somewhat resembled the leading man from the 1940s, except his hair was white and his eyes seemed to have disappeared into his face. His eyes stared out as if he was hiding within himself. As he neared the table the woman, Wanda, screamed at him:

"For Christ's sake, how many times have I told you to wipe your feet? Now, take your shoes off and put them outside!"

James did as he was told. Then walked back to the table in his stocking feet, sat down. Wanda had come to his 75th birthday party one evening with some of his friends and she had simply stayed. Now he didn't see much of his friends anymore. Wanda, who was 34 years younger, now handled his social affairs and his financial affairs. There had been sex between them at first but that had stopped years ago. James sat down to a plate of eggs and fried potatoes. Wanda sat across from him with a glass of sherry and lit a cigarette. She glared at James.

"Christ, I couldn't sleep last night! You were snoring again! I don't know what I'm going to do!"

The phone rang. It was there on the table next to

Wanda. Wanda always answered the phone.

"Yeh? This is the James Stagler residence. You're talking to Wanda Bradley, Mr. Stagler's agent. No, you can't speak to Mr. Stagler. What do you want? An interview for what magazine? What do you pay? I thought so, we don't give unpaid interviews."

Wanda banged the phone back into the cradle, glared at James again.

"Don't put so much *butter* on your toast! How many times do I have to tell you?"

James wasn't hungry. He liked to eat when it was quiet. It was seldom quiet. The phone rang again. Wanda snatched it up as if she were angry at it.

"Yes? Oh, Mr. Stanhouse. Listen, I told you, 500 grand if you want him in your movie ... yes, I *know* it's a cameo role! No, you can't speak to Jimmy! Yes, he's all right, he's fine, I see to that! Now, if you agree to the 500 thousand, bring over the papers and we'll dust him off."

Wanda put the phone down again, took a drink of her sherry.

"Eat your eggs! I didn't cook them for nothing!"

"I don't want to eat, Wanda."

"Eat those eggs!"

"No!"

"God damn you!"

Wanda stood up. She took her napkin and slapped James' face once and then again, hard.

James looked down into his plate of uneaten eggs. He spoke softly.

"I want you out of my house. I don't want you here ..."

Wanda just stood there. Then she laughed.

"Why, you old *fuck*! After all these years of taking *care* of you, you think I'm just going to walk out of here?"

"I'll give you the money ..."

"*You'll* give me the money? *I* handle the money around here."

"I don't want you here ..."

Wanda walked around the table and stood over him.

"Why you big *baby*! That's what you are, a big *baby*!" she laughed.

"I hate you," he said.

"You hate me, you ungrateful old man? Who cuts your hair, your toenails, pays your bills? Who makes your dental appointments? Who protects you from people? Who washes the shit out of your shorts? Who feeds you? You'd be dead in a week without me!"

James sat there over his eggs as Wanda stood there.

"I want to die," he said, "I don't care anymore ..."

"No use dying, old boy, you can still make us some money. I know Stanhouse is going to give us that half million. And all you have to do is say a few lines, or mumble a few. Anyhow, if you die now, you'll only go to hell."

"*This* is hell ..."

"Yeah, for *me*. Now, Jimmy, I'm telling you for the *last* time. *Eat those eggs!*"

James hated those eggs. They were dry and burned. He only felt like eating when he felt good and Wanda just stood there not understanding how or why he felt like he did. When he had first met her she had seemed so nice. She had laughed at everything he said, she had sat with him in the projection room while they watched his old films and she had said, "You were really better than Brando and a *hell* of a lot more man!" After his four wives and his endless girlfriends, Wanda had finally seemed the answer. But it had changed, it had changed all around.

He picked up the plate of eggs and threw them on the floor.

"*I won't eat these eggs!*"

Wanda stepped back a moment. She was a large woman with straight black hair, cut short. She stiffened and she smiled.

"Well, well, well. Look here, we have a bad boy here today, a *very* bad boy!"

Wanda walked over and finished off her sherry. Her

cigarette had gone out. She lit her cigarette. Then she walked to the kitchen closet. She came back with a whisk broom, a dustpan and a wastebasket. She stood over James with them and then suddenly threw them at him. They struck him, then clattered to the floor.

"Now!" she said, *"you clean up that mess!"*

James just sat there staring at the table. She stood over him. He could feel her there. Like something impossible. A pain gripped his throat, then his head. He sat there.

"Well," she said, "get *going!*"

Still, he sat there.

"Well, I'm not going to wait much longer!"

Then he said it:

"Go to hell!"

"*What? What did you say?*"

"I said, *go to hell!*"

Wanda leaped on him like a leopard. His chair fell backwards. She had a grip on his head and they rolled on the floor. She was partly on top of him, an arm locked around his head. Her strength surprised him. He could hardly breathe, but he could hear her:

"You old fool, you don't know the *misery* it's been living with you ..."

James couldn't breathe. It was getting worse. He felt that it was over for him and he didn't mind that except somehow he really resented it that it was at the hands of Wanda. Then he saw the fork on the floor. Then he had the fork in his hand and he plunged it into her back as hard as he could. Wanda screamed and leaped up. James scrambled to his feet. Wanda stood there trying to reach the fork in her back, screaming. It was in a place that she couldn't quite reach with either hand. She looked awful with that fork stuck in there and the blood coming down. Then she stopped screaming and just looked at him. She had the look of an animal in a trap.

"It's not going to kill you, Wanda," he said, "it's just a fork."

"Pull it out, Jimmy!" she commanded.

She turned her back to him and he stared at the fork sticking out there. It was firmly in place and the blood was flowing. He was surprised at all the blood. The blood made Wanda real again. It was like when they first met: she was human after all.

"Pull it out, Jimmy!"

"I will, Wanda, if you will promise me something ..."

"Just pull the fork out!"

He looked at the fork in her back. He remembered how they used to make love. How every day was a good day. How it felt so good to care for somebody again and how it felt so good to be loved again. How everything had seemed funny, there were so many things to laugh at. Why did it go away? He had never wanted it to go away.

"You've got to promise me something ..."

"All right, I *promise*! What is it?"

"If I pull the fork out will you go away and leave me alone?"

"I promise! Now pull it out!"

James grabbed the fork with both hands and pulled.

"Christ," he said, "it's really *in* there!"

"Pull, you son-of-a-bitch! You're the leading man, you're the movie star, remember?"

James remembered his movies and it gave him strength. The fork came out and he had it in his hand and he looked at it. Wanda whirled, furious, grabbed the fork and they stared at one another. Then she suddenly plunged it into his stomach. She pulled it out and jammed it in again and pulled it out. James fell to the floor holding his gut.

"Now we're even," he said helplessly, looking at her.

"You senile asshole!" she screamed. *"I always hated you and your movies!"*

She moved over him and jabbed the fork at his face. She pulled it back as he grabbed at his mouth with both hands. She stuck the fork into his stomach again. She leaped on him and rolled him over screaming, *"I hate you, I hate you!"*

Once more she jammed the fork into his stomach, pulled it out. Then she stopped. James lay very still, not looking at her, almost not breathing. She dropped the fork, got up and walked back to the table, sat down. She then saw his plate, his eggs, his potatoes on the floor. When she saw that, the anger left her. Her eyes became very wide and almost beautiful. With a rush a sudden remorse came over her. It was odd. Now, she cared for him. He had been a strange and a wonderful and famous man. He had gotten old. But that wasn't his fault. Now she didn't want the money. She only wanted him alive. She wanted him there with her. Far off she heard a dog barking. That dog was alive. When something was alive it was unique, exceptional, no matter what the circumstances.

Wanda inhaled, exhaled, very conscious of doing so. She didn't dare think of James.

The dog barked again.

She took the bottle, poured another sherry. She drank it down. She looked around. It was a beautiful house.

The phone rang. Wanda picked it up.

"Hello?"

It was Stanhouse. Stanhouse said it was okay about the half million. He was ready to come over with the papers when James could see him.

"I'm sorry, Mr. Stanhouse," Wanda said, "we've talked it over and James has decided to give up acting."

She hung up quietly.

Off in the distance the same dog barked again.

an evaluation

I've seen 70,000 horse races
and often
like this afternoon
as the horses slowly approached
the gate,
I thought, this is insanity,
I am murdering the hours,
I am tearing my heart out and
stamping on it with my
feet,
this is a madhouse,
this is towering stupidity,
this is death laughing at
me.
this is just another 8 hour
job.

they put them in the gate,
the sun came down,
a bell rang and they broke
from the gate
and were off down the
track,
and I thought, does it
really matter?
where's the glory here?
it's just repeat and
repeat and
repeat,
the grinding hours,
the routine.

it was a
business,
it was a
fake.

the game was getting old,
I was getting old.

they came around and into
the stretch,
the son-of-a-bitch, it was
the 7 horse, my horse,
drawing away at about 9-to-one.
I had a ten on it.
it paid $90.20.

I decided to stay for one more
race.
what would I do at home
at 3:30 in the
afternoon?

sleep?

I strolled toward the
payoff
window.

a fellow had to keep his
hand in the
action.

neon

today at the track they gave
all the patrons
neon caps.
the caps glowed and
said
HOLLYWOOD PARK.

some of those jerk-offs
wore their caps
backwards.

25 thousand neon
heads.

faces of
greed.
stone
faces.
faces of
horror.
blank wall
faces.

idiot eyes
under
neon.

fat white
stupefied
husbands and
wives.

Oakies with
blond hair.

screechers
preachers
poachers
punks ...

left-overs,
half-dead,
part
warm.

neon
neon.

cement
faces.
blithering
voices.

nothing.

neon over
nothing.

I thought I was
in hell.

maybe I was in
hell.

a day-glow
inferno of
festering
hell.

he saw me walking into the track and he stood
waiting, he was a jockey's agent and I only knew
him slightly
but then he moved toward me,
"Hey, Hank, I want to ask you something ..."
I stopped.
he said, "Listen, I know this fellow, he's a friend
of mine and he writes poems, really wonderful
poems ..."
"I can't help him," I said and began walking
off.
"Yes, you can, all you have to do is to get on the
telephone!"
"No, I can't ..."
I walked further off.
"WHAT IS HE SUPPOSED TO DO THEN?" he yelled.
"SEND HIS WORK TO A GOD-DAMNED PUBLISHER!" I
yelled back.
then I was up the escalator and that was
over.
if I ever owned a horse I would never use one of
his jocks.
meanwhile, I checked the tote.
my selection was reading 5-to-one.
nice way to right a day that had started
wrong.

the 3 horse clipped the heels of
the 7, they both went down and
the 9 stumbled over them,
jocks rolling, horses' legs flung
skyward.
then the jocks were up, stunned
but all right
and I watched the horses
rising in the late afternoon,
it had not been a good day for
me
and I watched the horses rise,
please, I said inside, no broken
legs!
and the 9 was all right
and the 7
and the 3 also,
they were walking,
the horses didn't need the van,
the jocks didn't need the
ambulance.
what a beautiful day,
what a perfectly beautiful day,
what a wondrously lovely
day—
3 winners in a
single race.

as we stand there before the purple mountains
in our stupid clothing, we pause, look
about: nothing changes, it only solidifies,
our lives crawl slowly, our wives deprecate
us.
then
we awaken a moment—
the animals are entering the track:
Quick's Sister, Perfect Raj, Vive le Torch,
Miss Leuschner, Keepin' Peace, True to Be,
Lou's Good Morning.

now, it's good for us: the lightning flash
of hope, the laughter of the hidden gods.
we were never meant to be what we are or where
we are, we are looking for an out, some music
from the sun, the girl we never found.
we are betting on the miracle again
there before the purple mountains
as the horses parade past
so much more beautiful than
our lives.

as the poems go

as the poems increase into the thousands you
realize that you've created very
little.

it all comes down to rain, the sunlight,
the traffic, the nights and the days of the
years, the faces.

leaving this will be easier than living
it.

typing one more line now as
a man plays a piano through the radio.

the best writers have said very
little
and the worst,
far too much.

the telephone

many women I have known have
been very much connected to
the telephone.
they can talk virtually for
hours.
it is their manner of
measuring where they
are or are
not.
some women have major
problems with aging
and with
men.
on the telephone they
speak of
real and imagined
injustice,
they let loose their
poison,
they justify their
beliefs and
positions.

my wife has been
speaking to one of her
gender
back east.
the conversation is
now proceeding
into its second
hour.

if a psychiatrist or
a psychologist
were listening
their notes would be
bulging with
references to
trenchant
instability and
gratuitous masturbation
of the
psyche.

but I am neither psychiatrist
nor psychologist.
I am just the poor son-of-
a-bitch who has to pay
the
phone bill.

a misogynist who
writes these
poems.

HIDEAWAY

Harry walked into the bar and found a stool alone. Nobody on either side of him. The bartender dragged his bloated body up and Harry ordered a scotch and water. The barkeep waddled off. He was wearing dark brown pants. His butt was wide, gross. Harry stared at the sagging buttocks, watched the wrinkles in the back of his pants. Then Harry glanced around. Nothing but lonely middle-aged guys who wanted to talk about the Rams or the Dodgers or something equally senseless.

The bartender came back with the drink. Harry paid him but the bartender kept standing there. He was wearing a faded blue t-shirt with a hole near the left shoulder. He leaned against the bar and his belly flopped over the wood. He kept looking at Harry and Harry could hear him breathing.

"What do you want?" Harry asked him.

"I wanna welcome ya to the Hideaway." The bartender grinned through his greasy lips.

"Thanks," said Harry.

The bartender reached under the bar and came up with a wooden cup. He grinned foolishly at Harry, shook the container up near his ear, lowered it and flipped out a pair of dice. "All the boys," he said, "are going to roll to see who buys the next round of drinks. Low number buys. You wanna join us?"

The conversation in the bar stopped. The juke box was silent. Harry noted that most of the patrons were dressed in dirty white t-shirts. Some of them were skinny, with long thin arms and the t-shirts hung from them like dirty rags. Others were fat or muscular and the t-shirts gripped them snugly, creeping up toward their armpits leaving their hairy bellies and bellybuttons exposed. One guy was dressed in a heavy jacket that was much too large for him. They all seemed to be waiting for his answer.

"No," Harry said, "count me out."

The barkeep turned and waddled back down to the guy at the end. They whispered a moment, then the bartender turned his head and looked back at Harry. The look was noncommittal. The first guy rolled the dice.

Harry belted his drink down.

The barkeep was moving from man to man. There was a high sense of glee in the place as each man rattled the container and spilled the dice out.

I wonder if a woman ever comes in here? thought Harry.

"Hey, barkeep!" Harry hollered.

The barkeep looked at Harry.

Harry raised his empty glass, winked, "How about a refill?"

The barkeep looked at Harry, inhaled, held it, then let it slowly come out. As he waddled toward Harry he snatched a bottle of scotch as if irritated. Then he stood there, pouring. Some of the scotch ran over his fat brown fingers as it poured into the shot glass. He dumped the shot in, added the water, then said to Harry, "You know, we got a great place here, everybody knows each other, everybody gets along."

"What do I owe you?" Harry asked.

"Same as before."

The barkeep took the money, made it down to the register, banged it open, slammed it shut. Then he went back to the dice. He moved along the bar, announcing the results of each roll. Finally he came down to the last patron, the guy dressed in the large jacket.

"Now, David," said the barkeep, "all ya gotta do is beat a 4, because Pee Wee threw a 4. Roll 'em, David!"

David rattled the dice in the wooden cup and let them go.

"*Holy shit!*" screamed the barkeep, "SNAKE EYES!"

It busted up the whole bar: fat guys and thin guys

started whooping it up and beating on the wood. One guy got going so bad he started to gag, couldn't get his breath. He bent over the bar and they beat on his back until he could breathe again.

Then it got quiet and the guy in the jacket reached into his wallet and flipped out some bills.

"It's all right," he said, "next time somebody else will be whistling Dixie out of his butthole."

The barkeep went about pouring refills. One of the fellows, one of the very thin ones, got up and put some money into the juke box. It was a song about "Bette Davis' Eyes."

"That Bette Davis, she was some woman," said one of the fellows.

"She's still alive," said another.

"Oh yeah?"

"She still was some woman."

"Yeah, but there was something evil about her."

"She was still a great actress."

"Maybe so."

The barkeep walked down to Harry, stood there.

"You all right?" he asked Harry.

"Yes."

"You had a fight with your woman?"

"Not really."

"What do you mean?"

"Nothing."

"I got to tell you something, mister. We don't like unhappy people around here. We get along."

"I'm not unhappy."

"Then what is it?"

"What do you mean?"

"I mean, you don't seem to be a friendly fellow."

"I'm sorry, I didn't mean to give that impression."

"We get along here. We all know each other."

"How about another drink?"

The barkeep waddled off, came back with the bottle:

216

"You know, we don't want trouble here. We're all peaceful people."

"O.K.," said Harry, "only this time don't add so much water."

"O.K.," said the barkeep, "by the way, what do you do?"

"What do I do? Right now, I'm drinking."

The barkeep leaned back a little from the bar.

"HEY FELLOWS!" he yelled.

All the white t-shirts looked toward them, plus the big jacket.

"I asked this gentleman what he did and you know what he told me? He said he *drank*!"

One of the white t-shirts applauded. The others joined in.

"All right!" one of them yelled, "He's one of us!"

The barkeep leaned toward Harry: "You play pool?"

"No, I was never any good at pool."

The bartender leaned closer. His belly was almost crawling across the bar and into Harry's drink.

"What're you good at?"

Harry laughed. "Well, hell, I guess I just don't excel at anything."

The bartender leaned closer: "Where you from? Newark? Kansas City?"

"Santa Fe."

"Wow! Santa Fe!"

The barkeep leaned back and raised his walrus head: "HEY YOU GUYS, THIS GUY IS FROM SANTA FUCK!"

The fellows didn't seem to pay so much attention to that.

The barkeep leaned forward again. "How come you came to this bar tonight?"

"No real reason. Give me a refill."

The barkeep poured it right into the glass, forgetting the water.

Harry drained the glass.

"O.K., I had a fight with my woman."

"You told me earlier that you didn't have a fight with your woman."

"I said, 'not really.' "

"What's that mean?"

"I mean, not really."

"So you just came in here because there was nowhere else to go?"

"I'm not knocking your place. I just didn't feel like going right home tonight."

Then the barkeep leaned back and stood there. He didn't look at Harry. He appeared to be looking at some place over Harry's head and to the left. He seemed to be in a reverie.

Then he leaned forward, leaned against the wood and looked at Harry.

"You been in the service?"

With that question it seemed as if the entire bar became very quiet.

"You mean the armed forces?"

"Yes."

"No."

"Everybody here's been in the service. Except for Pee Wee. He was too small."

Harry didn't answer.

The barkeep reared back and looked at the same spot over Harry's head. Then he leaned forward again.

"How come you didn't go?"

"I don't know. I guess I fell somewhere between Korea and Vietnam. I was never the proper age. Besides, what does it matter?"

The barkeep's stomach left the wood and he stood almost straight.

"Hey fellows!" he said in a loud voice. "HERE'S A GUY WHO SAYS ALL THE WARS WE FOUGHT IN DIDN'T MATTER!"

"He's got a pussy for brains," said one of the white t-shirts.

218

"All right," said Harry, "I'm leaving."

He got off his stool and started walking toward the rear exit. His car was in the parking lot back there. He was feeling all right. The drinks had helped.

As he neared the end of the bar, one of the white t-shirts stuck out a foot and tripped him. Harry lost his balance and almost crashed into the pinball machine. But he slammed his palms against the glass and righted himself.

Harry turned and walked over to the man who had tripped him. The man had nice blue eyes. On one of his thin arms was tattooed the message: BORN TO DIE. On the bar in front of the man stood half a drink. Harry reached over, picked the drink up, pulled the fellow's t-shirt open at the neck and poured the drink in.

He was drunker than he thought. He found the car, got the key, opened the door, got in, locked the door and here they came. The white t-shirts and the big jacket. The bartender was not with them.

Harry started the engine. They were all over his car like a swarm of drunken killer bees. Two were on the hood. One was on the roof. Two were attempting to roll the car over.

Harry put it into reverse and slowly backed out toward the alley. Several of the drunks were now pushing against the rear of the car. In the rearview mirror Harry saw one of them fall under the wheels. He hit the brakes and rolled down the window on the driver's side.

"Jesus Christ, get out of the way!"

A long thin arm came in through the window and tried to pull the keys from the ignition. Harry took the arm and bent it hard against the steering wheel. He heard the snap, there was a scream and the arm vanished back out of the window. Harry rolled the window up and continued backing out.

He backed and made a left turn toward the boulevard. There was a face pressed against the windshield, eyes leering in. He saw the hands, their fingers, clutching at the glass, frog-like useless things. Harry knew that once he was on the boulevard he could shake him free.

He roared up the alley. The man fell off the hood. At the last moment he spotted the sacrificial lamb, a fat white t-shirt spreading its arms and blocking the alley exit. Harry veered to the right, ramming a brown slat fence. The fence broke apart. There were slats and pieces of wood flying everywhere ...

Harry got back to his apartment, took off his clothing, his shoes. He sat there in his shorts for a few minutes and then walked to the refrigerator. Luck: 4 cans of beer left. He cracked one, brought it out and sat back down on the couch. He flicked the remote control, he got Johnny Carson.

Now, thought Harry, there is a man. If the whole world was like Johnny Carson there might be a chance.

Then he thought, that's wrong, Carson gets along too well with just anyone. He likes everybody.

Harry swallowed the last gulp of that can of beer and then the phone rang.

It was Lisa.

"Where have you been? I've been phoning you for hours! Where have you been?"

"Nowhere, really."

"You've been with some *slut*! I'm a woman! Women have a way of knowing these things! *You've been with some slut!*"

Harry hung up the phone, took the thing off the hook.

He had three cans of beer left.

With them and if he was careful he might make it to morning.

this dirty, valiant game

I see e. e. cummings drinking a
rum and tonic while sitting on
the front porch of a white
house.

I see Ezra at St. Liz
accepting visitors as a confirm-
ation of his existence.

I see Hart Crane on an
ocean steamer
rejecting the advances of
literary ladies while
lusting for the cabin
boy.

I see Hemingway clean-
ing his shotgun
while thinking of his
father.

I see Dostoevsky at the
roulette wheel
losing everything to
Christ.

I see Carson McCullers
dunking her beautiful
soul
in
whiskey.

I see Li Po
that wino
laughing at the
futility of word
following
word.

I see Sherwood
Anderson
swallowing the
toothpick that killed
him.

I see William
Saroyan
written-out,
sitting in his Malibu
beachfront home
waiting
vainly
for the luck to
return.

I see Timothy
Leary
going from
table to table
at parties
hoping to be
recognized.

I see Chattertor
purchasing the
rat poison,
I see Pascal
getting into the bath-

tub of warm water
with the
razor.

I see Ginsberg
gone
from Howling to
mewing
as a professor in
Brooklyn.

I see Henry
Miller
long stopped
writing,
putting adver-
tisements in a
college newspaper
for
secretaries.

I see Richard
Brautigan,
the age he high-
lighted past,
his books no
longer selling,
his love affairs
rotting, I can
see him blowing
himself away in
that mountain
cabin.

I see the
necessity of

creation, the love
of it, the danger of
it.
I can see where
creation often
stops while the
body still lives
and often
does not care
to.

the death of life
before life
dies.

Tolstoy sitting alone
in the
road.

all days night
forever.

flowers frozen in
blood
urine
wine.

stay out of my slippers, you fool

it's not good, some of the days we have, horrible
      dead-dog-in-the-
street days.
son-of-a-bitch, going on sometimes seems rather
useless.
read in the paper the other day,
a man fell into a meat grinder and was ground
up.
makes you think a bit about the gods.
like some things seem almost planned, worked out
        on some
drawing board.
it's fate, they say.
this man was born to die being ground to bits in
      a meat
grinder.
that was his main purpose.
they allowed him to do a few things first.
he'll be replaced.
somebody will take his job.
somebody will take your job
and mine.
your place and mine.
and the trees will shed their leaves
and the whores will sing in their showers
and the cats will sleep throughout the day
and the 20th century will click into the 21st
and somebody will throw away your shoes
and your belt and your old clothes and your
new clothes.
somebody will sleep in your bed.

somebody will throw a handful of dirt upon
you.

I get like this when I read about a man being
ground to death in a meat
grinder.
how do you feel?
what do you know?
get the hell out of my face!

the voice

we had a table outside
by the water,
it was a Saturday night,
all the tables were
filled.
we had finished eating,
we were drinking and
watching the freighters
and passenger ships
going by on their way to the sea
and Frankel was
talking.
I became very
conscious of his loud
voice.
I wasn't too
interested in what
he was saying
and neither were
the others,
but Frankel kept on,
he even got
louder,
he laughed, waved
his hands;
little pieces of
saliva flew from
his mouth.
heads were turning,
looking at us.

Frankel had been
told
in some distant
past
that he had a
great sense of
humor,
that he should
have been a
stand-up
comic.

he had 3 or 4
good lines but
we had
heard them all
before.

I finished my
drink, set it
down, managed
to reach out,
grab one of
Frankel's
flying hands.

I interrupted him
in mid-speech.

"listen, your voice,
can you lower it
just a
bit?"

"huh?
oh sure ..."

then he went
on.
he kept it low
for some
moments,
then,
something he
was saying
excited him,
and he was
back at full
volume.

we paid the bill
and got him
out of
there.

going back
Frankel
was in another
car
following us.

"I hope I didn't
hurt his feelings,"
I said to my
wife.

"I was about to
tell him
myself," she
answered.

back at our
place

Frankel
began talking
again.
there were 4
other people
and we
listened.
it wasn't so bad
because we
all knew him
and the house
was set far
back,
not too close
to the
neighbors.

but we had
6 cats and they
all ran off,
out through the
door,
or they jumped
out of the
window.

the night went
on and Frankel
expounded loudly upon
the strange and
funny things in
his life, what
he said to
somebody and
what they
replied.

he used different
voices for the
different
people.

well, the night
finally wound
down
and we said
goodbye to
Frankel and his
friend
at the doorway.

they both said
they had had
a good
time.

then they were
in their car
and backing
out the
drive.

we sat down
for a quiet
nightcap.

the silence was
glorious.
it seeped through
us and we began
to recover.

then the cats

returned
one by one,
looking around
cautiously,
lifting their feet
delicately.

life was returning
to normal.

nobody said
anything.

enough (had been)
said.

the bard of San Francisco

don't old poets ever
die?
this one fellow,
you can see him every
morning
in the coffeehouse
at his own table
sipping a white wine and
reading *The New York
Times.*
then he'll go down to
the pool for a
swim.
they say he has the most
beautiful blue eyes in
America.
he dashes off on little
trips to Paris and
Madrid,
then returns.

he still gives poetry
readings, reads
well, has no fear of
his audience.
he can impress them,
does, just for something
to do.

he is not embittered,
refuses to

gossip.

he wears all manner
of hats, caps, head
gear,
and whatever he
puts on,
he never looks
ridiculous.
rather, he looks
dashing, he looks
like royalty.
he's thin, he's
straight, he's
tall,
and if the sun is
shining anywhere,
it shines on
him.
and his books
still sell,
handsomely.

the male poets
talk about him,
they use much of
their time
talking about him
and
rather
unkindly.
the lady poets
adore him.
and the other
ladies
adore him.

he is often seen
with a new
woman.
he is very composed
about it
all.
and with death
looking over his
shoulder
he still manages
to write
decent
poetry.

on biographies

if you're dead
they don't
matter.

most biographers,
of course,
imagine things
about their
subjects
that aren't
true.

worse, they take
your jokes as
fact
and the other
way
around.

and in interviewing
ladies from your
past
they will accept
their
pronouncements
without
question.

biographies
about writers
are mostly

tomes of literary
gossip.

and if it is about
a living writer,
by then
he is often
almost physically
dead
and
in most cases
absolutely
spiritually
dead.

he will accept any
amount of praise,
ignore any
criticism,
congratulate his
biographer
on a job
well
done

and wonder
what
took them
so god-damned
long
to do
it,
anyhow.

a real break

I've heard it said that you
give a real lively
performance
and there really isn't
much going on
in this
town,
so we'll fly you
down,
put you up in a nice
hotel,
you can have
all you want to
drink,
we can rent this
hall,
it holds a real
bunch,
and you'd be
surprised
how many people
around here
know about
you,
we'll pack them
in
and we promise
you
25% of the
gate.

we love you,
man!
how about
it,
huh?

avoiding humanity

much of my life has been dedicated
to just that.

and still is.

even today at the track,
I was sitting alone between races,
in a dumb dream-state
but dumb or not,
it was mine.

then I heard a voice.
some fellow had seated himself
right behind me.

"I've come where it's nice and
quiet," he said.

I got up, walked about 150 yards
away and sat down
again.

I felt no guilt, only the return of a
more pleasant state of
being.

for decades I have been
bothered by door-knockers,
phone-ringers, letter-writers; and
strangers in airports and bars,
boxing matches, cafes, concerts,

libraries, supermarkets, jails,
hospitals, hotels, motels,
pharmacies, post offices,
etc.

I am not a lonely person.
I don't want to be embraced, cajoled,
told jokes to, I don't want to share
opinions or talk about the
weather and/or etc. and
etc.

I have never met a lively, original
interesting soul by accident and
I don't expect to.

all I have ever met are a herd of
dullards who have wanted to project
their petty frustrations upon me.

for some time women fooled
me.
I would see a body, a face, a
seeming aura of peace and
gentleness, a cool refreshing lake
to splash in,
but once they spoke
there was a voice like
chalk scratching a blackboard,
and what came forth as
speech
was a hideous and crippled
mind.

I lived with dozens of these.

wait.
the phone is ringing now.
but I have a message
machine.
they are leaving
one.

this one wants to see
me.
it wants to invite
itself over.
a reason is given,
some pretense.
it is hardly a worthy
one.
the last words are,
"Please let me know."

why do they want to see
me?
I don't want to see
them.
can't they sense
this?

am I the only one in the
world who finds being
alone to be a blessing, a
miracle?

must I always be kind to
those who would wallow
in my hours?

am I an ugly soul?
unkind?

unappreciative?
misanthropic?
a misogynist?
a crackpot?
a bastard?
a murderer of hope?
do I torture animals?
am I without love?
do I reek of bitterness?
am I unfair?
am I the wrecking ball of dreams?
am I the devil's encore?
do I put glass in the sandbox?
am I without morals or mercy?

if so, why do they want to keep
seeing me?

I would never want to see
anybody like that.

especially
when I am
shaving.

What Happened to the Loving, Laughing Girl in the Gingham Dress?

Harry reached over and switched off the table lamp. It had been a wasted night: nothing on tv as usual, nothing to read. It was 12:30 a.m. At least, he hadn't gotten drunk. But maybe he should have. At least that would have been an accomplishment. But some nights you just wasted, and some days and some weeks and some years. He'd had some rough years but here he was, still alive, and some might even consider him a financial success but money meant little to him. He had no desire for possessions, trinkets, travel. One thing he liked was solitude and another thing he liked was the absence of trouble of any kind. Harry had had more than his fill of trouble. At times, when he looked back, it was amazing to him that he was still alive. But there were many lives such as his, he was sure of that.

Well, sleep had always been one of his favorite escapes. Sleep was the grand healer, the equalizer. Harry slept well, he slept almost with a vengeance.

Harry noted the full moon through the window, closed his eyes, inhaled, exhaled. A man didn't really need too much. Just some ease of mind, a gentleness for the spirit. He was almost asleep when the phone rang. He turned on the table lamp, picked up the receiver. It was Diana.

"I've got a flat tire! Jesus Christ, I don't know what to do! I've got a flat tire! I decided to go to the 7-11 for some cat food and I got this god-damned flat!"

"Listen," Harry said, "you've got your Auto Club card. Phone them and they'll come out and change your tire."

"I've tried, I've tried!" Diana screamed. *"I keep getting a busy signal or they put me on hold! And when you finally get through to them it takes them hours to come! I'm terrified! A gang of*

244

guys drove by in a car and hollered at me! I might get raped!"

"Look," Harry said, "just phone the Auto Club once more. I've always had luck with them. Ten or fifteen minutes at the most. Meanwhile, I'll get dressed and come over."

"I'm not going to call them again! I've used up all my change! This is the last call I can make!"

There was some further cursing interspersed by screams. At the first opportunity Harry spoke.

"Listen, I told you I was coming over. It will be all right. Please calm down."

"But you don't know where I am! How are you going to find me?"

"Tell me where you are."

"But you have no sense of direction! You're always getting lost! How are you going to find me?"

"I'll find you. Tell me where you are."

"I'm on Ocean Street!"

"I know where that's at. That's where you live."

"I'm not near where I live! I'm on a different part of Ocean Street!"

"What's the nearest cross street?"

"Sepulveda! Do you know where Sepulveda is?"

"Of course."

"You asshole, you've been living in this area for years and you probably don't know where Sepulveda is!"

"I'll get there. Sepulveda and Ocean. I'll find you."

"But you don't know what corner I'm on!"

"Don't worry. I'll see your car."

"Tell me exactly how you're going to get here!"

"I'll take Western to Pacific Coast Highway, take a left, then take a right on either Crenshaw or Hawthorne, drive until I hit Sepulveda, take a left and go until I hit Ocean."

"Do you know where Lomita is?"

"The street or the city?"

"The street, you asshole!"

"I thought you were at Sepulveda and Ocean?"

245

"I am! But Lomita is the first street you come to before you get to Sepulveda!"

For a moment Harry felt like hanging up. Instead he said, "All right, I'm coming over but after I get you out of this one, I never want to see you again. You got that? *This is it!*"

There was a long scream. Then:

"No, no, no! I'm going to kill myself! I'll kill myself right now!"

Diana screamed again. When she finished and began to sob Harry said, "All right, I didn't mean it. I'm sorry. I'll be right out. I have to get dressed first."

Diana reverted right back to her old self. *"All right, do you know exactly where I am?"*

"Yes, I'll find you. Now, calm down. We can fix this whole thing."

"Oh, you asshole!"

"Now what is it?"

"It's just that you're so fucking calm!"

"Listen, Diana, I'll be right over. I'm going to hang up. I'm on the way."

Harry picked his shorts up off the floor, got into them, got into his pants, his shoes without stockings, then stopped at the refrigerator, got a beer, uncapped it, drank it. It went down like a thimbleful. Then he went in and forced a piss so that he wouldn't have to piss on Sepulveda, made his way to the car and drove off.

As he drove up Western he looked at the people in other cars. They seemed quite rational. It was all very strange. Almost every woman he had ever dated had done time in a madhouse, or had madness in the family, brothers in jail, sisters who suicided. Harry drew these types to him. Even in the schoolyards, the mad and the strange and the misfits had been drawn to him. It was his curse. But he didn't have the cure, he just had the problem. And Diana was an extremist. Each time she got ill, she thought she was dying. She would scream and rant. "Jesus Christ," Harry had told her once, "when I was on my god-damned deathbed I didn't make all this fuss. All you can do is die." The message had been wasted.

Finally he was on Sepulveda. That was a relief. Sometimes Diana almost had him believing his own assholeness. Harry drove along, watching for Ocean. Then he saw the car. An Alfa Romeo. He had purchased it for Diana. Sky blue. Diana loved sky blue. He pulled up and parked behind the Alfa Romeo. There was no movement within the car. He opened his door, got out, walked up to the car. Diana was sitting there, staring straight ahead. Harry knocked on the window. Diana rolled it down.

"O.K.," Harry said, "I'm going to phone the Auto Club. I'll be right back."

"You're not going to leave me here! I'm going with you!"

She leaped from the car door, stood on the pavement, hair in eyes, hands dangling oddly.

"No, wait! We're not going to phone the Auto Club. It takes them hours! We can do it ourselves!"

Diana ran to the back of the car, came back with a tiny jack, plus a lug wrench about the size of an ordinary can opener. Harry tried the lug wrench, knowing ahead of time that it was useless. The nuts were frozen. They'd probably been tightened with an electric lug wrench. Harry got his own lug wrench and tried it on the wheel. It didn't fit.

"We're going to have to phone the Auto Club," Harry said.

"Why the fuck do they make stupid wrenches like that? Why is everybody so fucking stupid?"

"Come on, let's try a phone booth."

They started to cross Sepulveda when an old car with four young guys waving beer cans drove by and let out a yell. So Diana hadn't imagined it after all. Harry only hoped that they would come back so he could bang their heads together. But they didn't. It wasn't Harry's lucky night.

Harry got the Auto Club on the phone. He had Diana's

card in his hand. He gave the lady the location of the car, the problem and the Auto Club identification number.

"Is the lady there?" Harry was asked.

"She's here but I'm phoning for her."

"I can hear her," said the Auto Club lady. "Would you mind putting her on the phone?"

Diana had been cursing and offering instructions from the background.

"Is that necessary?" Harry asked the Auto Club operator.

"Yes, I wish to speak to the lady ..."

Harry handed the phone to Diana, thinking, oh shit, they'll never come now. We're finished.

"He told you where we were! How many fucking times do we have to tell you? No, I don't know the number! There aren't any street numbers! It's a deserted area! Where am I now? I'm outside a Thrifty drugstore in a phone booth! No, I don't know the number of the Thrifty drugstore! Your driver can find it! Thrifty Drugs! No, I'm not going to stay here! It's too cold! I'm going to wait in the car!"

Diana let go of the receiver and it dangled from the cord. Harry picked up the receiver in order to pacify the Auto Club. The line was dead.

"That cunt!" Diana screamed.

"Come on," Harry said, "let's go back to the car."

They crossed Sepulveda and Harry put Diana in the car. She was still ranting about the Auto Club. Harry walked out to the curb and lit a cigarette, waiting, somehow, for an Auto Club tow truck which might never arrive. All the dispatcher had to do was to take offense and not put in the call. Harry hoped the lady had a good soul. As for Harry, he'd give anything to be sitting in front of his tv with a beer, watching a replay of "The Honeymooners." If only a man could pack off to some city in Canada and never be seen or heard from again. But it was never that easy. You were destroyed by what you befriended.

Harry lit another cigarette and walked up and down.

Then came a great surprise! An Auto Club tow truck came rolling along! Harry jumped and waved. The guy saw him and pulled up. Such a beautiful sight. If there was proof of God it was the arrival of an Auto Club truck in the middle of the night.

The man got out of the truck and approached the Alfa Romeo. Diana leaped out.

"We couldn't get the wheels off with this stupid wrench! Why do they make stupid wrenches like this?"

The man didn't answer. Then he said, "You've got *two* flat tires."

"Oh," Diana said, "I hadn't noticed. When I hit that fucking traffic island I felt the tire blow. I didn't know it was two."

Ah, Christ, Harry thought, this nightmare is endless.

"Well, I don't know what I can do," said the Auto Club man.

"Just go ahead and put on the spare," said Harry. "Maybe I'll think of something. Better one flat than two."

Then Diana couldn't find her car keys. There was more major hysteria. Then she found the keys—in her purse.

The Auto Club man found the spare in the trunk, brought it out, said, "There's no air in this spare. Somebody has let it go down."

The man brought out an air tank and inflated the spare. The spare went down again.

"This spare is flat," said the man.

For once, Diana was silent.

Three flat tires.

"Well, shit," Harry laughed, "let's just blow up the fucking car and leave it here."

"No, wait," said the Auto Club man, turning to Diana.

"You live near here?"

"Yes, about a mile."

"Well, I can tow your car to your place and leave it there."

"Can you do that?" said Diana. "That would be just fine."

More endless nightmare upon endless nightmare, thought Harry, no, no, no, no.

"No," said Harry, thinking, "there's a tire place about 4 or 5 blocks from here. Let's just haul the car down there and we'll fix it in the morning."

"That's O.K. with me," said the Auto Club man. "I know where that place is."

"Shit," said Harry, "let's do it." He and Diana climbed into the tow truck.

The Auto Club man towed the car to the tire shop and then he left. The Alfa Romeo with its flat tires was parked directly in front of the building.

"Now," Harry said, "we can leave one note on the windshield under the wiper and we'll leave another note under the office door. Then they can't miss it."

"What'll I write?" Diana asked.

"Tell them you need tires. That we'll be back in the morning. Leave your phone number and mine."

Diana got some sheets of paper out of her car and laid them on the hood of the Alfa Romeo and began writing. She wrote for a long time. Then she handed the sheets to Harry. Each sheet was 18 or 20 lines long. Harry had no idea what she had written. He took one sheet and placed it under the wiper and then walked to the office door with the other sheet.

"What are you doing?" Diana screamed. *"Put it in the mail slot!"*

"No," said Harry, and he slid it under the door, face up, so they would see it. Every edge against possible misunderstanding was needed.

Harry got Diana back to her place. He told her that in the morning he'd be back, he'd get her some new tires, and then everything would be all right.

When he got back to his place it was 4:35 a.m. Not too

late. He uncorked a bottle of good wine and had a large glassful. Then he had another. It went down well and it was needed. It was cowardly, of course, to attempt to forget the incomprehensible, but nevertheless it was necessary.

In the morning Harry phoned the tire shop and told them he'd be over to purchase tires for the Alpha Romeo. "Fine," said the man, "we got your letters."

Harry got to Diana's about ten a.m.

As he approached her open doorway she must have heard him coming.

"Oh my God! My God! I can't stand it! I want to die!"

He walked in.

"What is it, Diana?"

"I can't leave this place like this!"

"What is it?"

"Can't you see? There's piss and shit all over the floor! The toilet backed up!"

"Well, we'll clean it up."

"The toilet's stopped up and I don't have a plunger! And I've got nothing to clean the floor with! I can't leave!"

This is Saturday, thought Harry, if I don't get her car fixed it'll be there until Monday and there will be further complications.

"I'll get you some stuff," said Harry.

"Where are you going? Where are you going?"

"I'll be right back," said Harry.

Where the hell can I buy some towels? he thought as he drove along.

He saw a large department store, parked, got out. The doors were just opening. He walked in with the customers who had been waiting.

Harry found the towel department. He grabbed three of the largest towels and put them on his VISA card. He had a hangover.

He asked the lady where he could get a plunger.

"Hardware," she said. "Two aisles to the left and one down ..."

Harry walked around to the Hardware section. There were no plungers on display. There were no clerks in the Hardware section. He went over to Automotive where the clerk saw him coming, turned his back and walked off. He cornered the clerk at the dead end of an aisle.

"Listen, don't they have a clerk in the Hardware section?"

"I don't think so."

"Don't they have any plungers in this store?"

"They should be in Hardware."

"There's nothing there."

"They must be on order."

Harry left the store and drove around some more. Then he saw Thrifty Drugs. He parked and went in. It was a hot morning and the hangover made him sweat excessively. He saw some plungers. But it was madness. They were tiny. They only cost a dollar. Maybe I can make it do until I find another, he thought. He purchased the little plunger and went back to Diana's.

"Here," he said, "some towels and a plunger."

"Oh, Jesus Christ, I can't use that plunger! Oh, I feel like dying!"

Then she screamed. When she finished Harry said, "I'll be right back."

"Where are you going?"

"I'll be right back."

"Oh, all this mess! What will I do?"

"I'll be right back."

Harry jumped into his car and drove off again. He saw a home appliance store, parked, went in. He found a plunger! A beautiful black plunger! He paid cash and took it back to the car.

Back at Diana's he said, "Here's a real plunger! Look!"

Diana grabbed it.

"Wait, I'll do it," suggested Harry.

252

But Diana already had the plunger and she was working at the toilet. She sobbed as the water splashed about. She stopped to flush the toilet, then worked the plunger again. The dark water rose to the edge of the toilet and Harry thought, oh, my God. Then, at the last moment, the water whirled down and away. The toilet was clear.

"There," he said, "we've solved that."

"I can't go!" Diana screamed. *"I can't clean this floor! I don't know what to do! What will I do?"*

"You've got the towels."

"I can't use those beautiful towels on the floor!"

"What do you need?"

"Paper towels!"

"I'll be right back ..."

Harry jumped into his car and went back to Thrifty Drugs. He found the paper towels. He got several different types of paper towels. Then he went back to Diana's. What can she say now? he thought.

"I can't clean the floor, oh God, I can't clean the floor!"

"Why, what's wrong?"

"I don't have any soap! How can you clean the floor without soap!"

"I thought maybe you had some soap."

"I don't have any soap!"

"I'll be right back."

The hangover seemed to be getting worse. He jumped into the car, lit a cigarette, gagged. Then he drove back to Thrifty Drugs. He got three different brands of soap. The same girl was at the cash register, but she didn't recognize him. Or maybe she did and thought he was mad.

Then he was back at Diana's with the soap.

"I'm going to get a newspaper," he told her.

He jumped back into his car, went back to Thrifty Drugs and got a newspaper out of the rack in front. Then he returned. He sat in a chair outside and read the newspaper. His mouth was very dry and he was ill to the stomach. He read the front section, the feature section, the sports section.

Then he heard Diana. "As soon as I shower we'll go."

"O.K." he said ...

The Alfa Romeo sat there with its flat tires and Harry went to the office to get things moving. There would be 3 new tires needed and put the most worn tire in the trunk for the spare, thank you.

The clerk seemed very understanding.

"Come back in an hour and your car will be ready."

They walked down to the Sizzler and they got the Hibachi chicken, the Double-Hibachi chicken. Diana also had a salad and an iced tea. Harry had a coffee. The place was crowded.

"Eat slowly," said Harry, "we've got an hour."

Somehow they managed to kill an hour. Harry drank much more coffee than he felt like drinking. He felt as if he was going to puke.

They walked back to the tire shop. The car stood there, untouched, still on its flat tires.

Harry went back to the nice clerk.

"They haven't touched the car," Harry told him.

"They haven't?"

The clerk left the counter and shouted through the door, "HEY, EDDIE, BRING THAT ALFA UP HERE, WILL YOU?"

The clerk turned to Harry, "Sorry sir, we'll get right on it!"

"Let's wait in my car," Harry suggested to Diana.

They walked to the car and sat and waited. Still, nobody moved the Alfa. There were various men about in their white uniforms. Some drank coffee. Others stood and smoked, talking to each other. Another was on the telephone.

Then from out of nowhere came a fat man in his white uniform. He got into the Alfa Romeo and started the motor.

"What's he going to do?" Diana screamed.

"He's going to move your car over to the rack," said Harry.

254

"He can't drive it like that! He can't drive it on those tires. He'll ruin the rims! Tell him to stop!"

"It's just a short distance. The rims will hold up."

The fat man slowly drove the car toward the rack.

"He's ruining my car! Make him stop!"

Harry put his head down and stared at the floorboard. He didn't want to stop him.

When he looked up the car was parked near the rack. He saw the fat man get out and walk off. The fat man was gone for 5 minutes. When he came back he had a sandwich in one hand and a large Coke in the other. He walked past the Alfa and out a side door and was gone. Harry started to open the door to go back to see the clerk in the office.

"Don't bother them, they might resent it," said Diana.

"Maybe you're right."

They sat there. In another ten minutes a thin man appeared. He rolled up 3 new tires.

"Tell him not to use the electric lug wrench to put the tires on," said Diana.

Harry walked over and told the thin man that.

"O.K." said the man.

Harry walked back to the car. The thin man changed one wheel, then walked off.

Oh my God, thought Harry. This is most surely the day I am being tested, to see if I am ready for the other world.

Then the thin man was back smoking a very long cigarette.

"Hey, Monty," he yelled to somebody, "what are you doing tonight?"

"We're double-dating," came the answer from somewhere. "We're going to Orion's. Do you know where Orion's is?"

"Sure, I know where Orion's is!"

Then, suddenly, music came out over the loudspeakers. It was loud, quite loud. A woman was singing, only you couldn't make out the words. The music stayed on. The song ended and a man began singing. Harry really felt like puking.

Twenty minutes of song. Then the thin man yelled at them over the music.

"O.K., IT'S READY!"

This is it, thought Harry, victory at last! We have endured. We have come through. We have surmounted all.

Harry walked into the office and paid the bill. He felt great. He joked with the clerk. He loved the clerk. All men were brothers. The world was fine. He was free.

He walked back to Diana.

"Well, you've got a new car. 3 new tires. And you've got a new paint job from last week and a new top from the week before. Your car looks great."

Diana got into her car and started it up.

"Thanks," she said, "and I'm sorry for everything. Things have been so fucked-up lately."

"Forget it. Everything's straight now. Happy driving. I'll phone you later. I'm going home to sleep for a couple of hours."

"Thanks again ..."

"O.K., kid, see you later."

Diana drove off toward the exit. She gave a little wave. Harry waved back.

Then she stopped at the street exit. She started honking her horn and staring tearfully at him through the driver's side window.

Harry ran up.

"What's wrong?"

"I'm sorry but I can't drive this car this way!" she said through the window.

"What is it?"

"There's this scraping sound! Listen!" She drove forward a few feet.

It was true. You could hear it over the music.

"Back it in again," Harry told her.

Harry went to the thin man and explained the scraping sound.

256

"Oh, we'll fix that right up," he said. "It's a minor adjustment."

The thin man took off the wheel that had been scraping, looked at it, put it back on. No scraping now.

Diana got in again and drove toward the exit. She waved, he waved. Harry inhaled and waited. The Alfa Romeo pulled into traffic and was gone.

Harry got back to his place, took a bath and had a beer. He got lucky. There was a good middleweight fight on tv. He was still alive. The late afternoon sun came through the window and bathed him in its glory. Things were coming together. He made an egg sandwich with green peppers. In an hour or so he phoned Diana.

"Everything all right?" he asked.

"Yes," she said, "but I've been worried about my cat. Those males have been terrorizing her, those sons-of-bitches. But she's here now. She's all right."

"Great ..."

"Mother just called. She's coming to visit next week just as planned. And she says to thank you again for letting her stay in your spare bedroom. You have such a lovely home."

"It's all right ..."

"She's only going to stay 3 days, then she's going north."

"O.K."

"I've got her arrival time at the airport and all that. You know she's getting along in years. Last week she broke a bone in her foot coming down a stairway. She might be in a wheelchair."

"We'll take care of her," said Harry.

"I want to get some blinds for her bedroom. You can see right in there from the street, that's not right."

"O.K."

"And thanks again."

"Forget it."

They said goodbye for the time being. Harry went and got another beer, then went outside and sat on the steps and smoked a cigarette. It was getting dark. Harry liked it dark. The darker the better. He smoked his cigarette and gulped at his beer. For the first time in 18 or 19 hours he felt pretty good. Pretty damned good. And he allowed himself the full enjoyment of that. He felt he had it coming. Darkness and peace. Ah, ah, ah ...

the luck of the word

throughout the years
I have gotten letters
from men
who say
that reading my
books
has helped them
get through,
go on.

this is high praise
indeed
and I know what
they mean:
my nerve to go
on was helped
by reading
Fante, Dostoevsky,
Lawrence, Celine, Hamsun
and others.

the word
raw on the page,
the similarities of
our hells,
when it all comes
through with
special
force,
those words and
what they speak

of
do help
get our asses
through the
fire.

a good book
can make an almost
impossible
existence,
liveable

for the reader
and
the writer.

bad form

the famous actor sat at the table with
his friends and the friends of the owner
of the horse
who was to run in the big race.
everybody had purchased tickets on the
owner's horse.

they sat together and watched the
race.
the owner's horse ran
badly, he ran
last.

some moments passed,
then the famous actor took his
stack of tickets
and tossed them down in front of the
owner.

they were spread there upon the white
tablecloth.

I no longer liked any of the movies
I had seen the famous actor
in.
I no longer liked the famous
actor.

I left the table.
I left the Director's Room.
I took the elevator down and out of

there.

I walked across to the
grandstand area
to where the non-famous
poor people were

and they were beautiful,
they had faces like
flowers
and I stared at them,
drinking in their
voluptuous
normalness.

last call

this is it, sucker, the dead nightingale
in your lap, the final circle around
the mirage, the bones of your dreams
buried, laughter caught in the speci-
men bottle, the caked blood of your
little paintings, the Hunter sighs,
the lynx huddles in the dark,
parsnip fingers grip the bottle,
old ladies mail you postcards from
Illinois,
as one fly circles the room and one room
circles the fly.
phone messages from the persistent:
old memories crushed in your brain
with hanging tongues;
the hammerhead shark dressed as a
nun;
2,000 years like a spider sucking at a
webbed insect;
the sodomized headless horse of
History;
the grandmother's smile;
Persistent Madness Syndrome
as a spiritual occupation;
mares eating oats and oats eating me
as the fleas play tambourines;
suicide as the last serenade to the
curse of Time;
the legless spirit flung against the
wall like
a bottle of vinegar;

the cat with 3 eyes walking through
the nightmare melody;
roasted pigs that cry in the heart
of a dog
walking north;
my aunt spitting out her paperclip
soul through the open window of
a 1938 Ford driving along Colorado
Boulevard;
Brahms talking to me as I lay a
20 dollar bet on the
6 horse;
the majesty of the club-footed duck
looking for the blocked
exit;
the applause of the terrified masses;
the last torn card upside down
in the ringing of an empty
room;
the last bluebird flying from the
burning
funhouse;
an apricot seed challenging the
sun;
the sheets of the whore raised
as a flag by political
centipedes;
zero times zero times zero
times zero;
the face in your mirror is love
drowned alone;
eating an apple is eating
yourself standing on a corner;
the paperclip speaking;
an onion more beautiful than
you;

Spain in your coffee cup;
the white horse standing on
the hill;
the dream stuffed in the
trash and the trash stuffed
in
you;
the beginning and the end
are the same;
the new gods imagined and the
old gods re-invented;
the human voice being the most
ugly instrument;
the falcon swirling and the vulture
swirling and the girls dancing with
eyes so blank;
everywhere the trees and plants
and flowers watching us
as their sadness towers tall
in the mighty night;
they weep and they weep
and they
weep;
the horse running last into
snow-covered mountains
as Li Po smiles
and bitter people
tear up their paper tickets
and blame the horse
and blame the life
and blame the blame
as the mountains weep
and the cross comes down
and lifts the sun;
the great white shark sniffing
the dark purple sea

as the mouse
alone
stares through its eyes at
all the
terror;
we burn separately and
together
in the December of our
undoing;
the walking blood of our
screams unrecorded
anywhere
but in our singular
private hells;
we dance when we can
we dig for worms and
coffins
we swim
we walk
we talk
we fornicate,
we gag
we gargle
we fish and
are
fished
hooked
caught
cleaned
fried
baked
broiled
simmered
eaten
digested
expelled;

it's a long wash
in and out of shore
through small lights and long darkness;
the bluebird
the bluebird
the bluebird
the chair in the center of the room with
nobody in
it;
everything waiting for the silver sword;
a piano playing somewhere
one small note at a time
a bluebird on each key;
my 6 cats asleep in the other room
waiting for me;
death only means something to
death;
it's late now
as the walls kiss me and hold me
and you
and you
and you
this terrible glory
as the Hunter himself almost wearies of
the hunt
but not
quite
not quite
not

not

quite.

well, you know, he started out as a
comedian
and then it was decided to make
him into a serious
actor,
the public always like that.
and then we decided to make him
politically aware,
we got him to pitch
all the right causes.
then Publicity sent out a story:
how he pulled a woman from a
wrecked car,
how he contributed large sums
to various charities while asking
that his name not be
revealed,
how he was going to give this
Benefit or that Benefit,
donating his time and
talent,
how he saved a child from
drowning,
how he did this and that.
we worked our asses black
and blue to create his
Public Image,
we were just starting to reap
a profit,
then, what happens?
the son of a bitch gets

drugged,
runs his Mercedes off a
cliff near Malibu
and kills
himself.

we couldn't do much with
that one.
we claimed some communists
who disliked some of his
causes
had messed with his
brake cables.

that took pretty well
but all in all
we finally had to write him
off
as a dead loss.

we got a new one now,
found some boy
working behind a fish
counter.
Tom is perfect:
totally bland features,
even a few
freckles,
large empty eyes
and a dog-like
grin.
he's a bit
addled,
but the clay's all there,
we'll shape him into
what they think they

need.

only with this one
we're going to use a
new twist, we are going to
start him as a serious
actor
and then turn him into
a comedian.

we're thinking all the time
here,
that's what makes
Hollywood
what it
is.

upon reading a critical review

it's difficult to accept
and you look around the room
for the person they are talking
about.

he's not there
he's not here.
he's gone.

by the time they get your book you
are no longer your
book.
you are on the next page,
the next
book.

and worse,
they don't even get the old books right.
you are given credit for things you don't
deserve, for insights that aren't
there.

people read *themselves* into books, altering
what they need and discarding what they
don't.

good critics are as rare as good
writers.
and whether I get a good review or a
bad one
I take neither

seriously.

I am on the next page.
the next book.

Paris, what?

you want to get stiffed? he asked
me, well, just send something to
the *Paris Review*, they have
their own select crowd of boys and
girls, it's a special club, you've
got to stink just right.

is that so? I sneered.

he drove off in his lambskin
Caddy
and I walked into the next
room,
looked at my 6 cats asleep
on the bed,
there was enough Power there
to crack the Universe
like a
walnut
shell.
I could taste it with the tips
of my ears,
I could see it through my
dark-stained
shorts.

the *Paris Review* ain't crap
to me,
I thought.
I was at the track today and
I picked 6 out of

nine
with agony stuffed in my
pockets
and the sun
behind a film of
pain.

I took a crap, then put
on Brahms'
2nd,
sent
this
one.

a social call

to suffer the fanged indifference of the
interloper
slurping beers at your
coffeetable,
if you asked this unquestionable
bore
to leave the premises
then your wife would forever
brand you as a mean and ugly
human
and so you measure your
choices
and decide to wait out the
boor
as he lights his cigarettes and
slurps his beer
talking on and on about
absolutely nothing
as the very walls yawn
as the rugs twist in agony
as the good hours are
uselessly murdered
as you consider,
this is what it must be like in
hell.
not flames and the devil
but just some fellow
fair of heart
and good enough in his own
way
talking about the mundane

variables,
going on,
caught in the mystery of his own
voice,
slurping the beer,
lighting the cigarettes
while Time is taking the 8-count,
while Time is being mugged.

some day you will be on
your deathbed
wondering why you
wasted it
all

as you now listen and
listen and listen,
in a hell before hell,
the palaver seeping to
your marrow.
when you are unkind
to yourself
you will know no
worse.
and deserve no
better.

the girls we followed home

the girls we once followed home are
now the bag ladies,
or one of them is that white-haired
old crone who
whacked you with her
cane.
the girls we once followed home
sit on bedpans in nursing
homes,
play shuffleboard at the public
park.
they no longer dive into the
white-capped waves,
those girls we followed home,
no longer rub their bodies with oil
under the sun,
no longer primp before the
beautiful mirror,
those girls we followed home,
those girls we followed home
have gone somewhere,
some forever,
and we who followed them?
dead in wars, dead of heart
attack,
dead of yearning,
thick of shoe and slow of
speech,
our dreams are tv dreams,
the few of us,
so few of us remember

the girls we followed home.
when the sun always seemed to
be shining.
when life moved so new and
strange and wonderful
in
bright dresses.

I remember.

slow starter

by the time I got good with things
other people were into
something else.
from the worst baseball player
I became the best,
unbelievably swift in the field,
tremendous power at the
plate
but by then the others were into
schooling, books, getting ready
for the future.
from a sissy I developed into
one of the best fighters
around
but by then
there was nobody left to
fight.

the girls took me even longer.
by the time I became an
expert lover
all of my compatriots were
either married
or disillusioned by the
chase.
all that was left for me were
the leftovers, the uglies,
the divorced, the mad, the
ladies of the
streets.

I always became the best
at things when those things
no longer counted:
football, high-speed driving,
drinking, gambling, clowning,
debating, bullshitting, going
to jail, going crazy, lifting
weights, shadow boxing with
fate.

but I was alone.
the others had become sedate,
had become responsible
citizens with
children, jobs, mortgages,
life insurance and pet
dogs.

the very things which terrorized
me.

I was the retarded child
still looking for more
childhood.
I still wanted to play but
there were no
playmates.

I bummed the country,
prowled the avenues,
the bars.
I found nothing, I
found
nobody.
I searched the skid
rows

thinking that something
could be hiding
there.
I thought
wrong.

being a late starter
also makes you late for heaven
or hell,
you are always trying to
catch something,
catch up to something,
some tangent, some
invisible thing,
it has to be there,
I can feel it there,
I see it sometimes in the eyes
of a tired old waitress,
or the round spot on a pillow
where the cat has
slept.

it's there and it beats the
funeral parlors
and the millions of feet
walking in their
shoes
and the way it seems to
be,
the cities, the faces, the
newspapers, the sidewalks,
the stop signs, the churches,
the flags and the
calendars, the whole
unholy act.

this childhood on the
hunt,
this late starter,
this slugger, this drunkard
is still on the
look-out
and I know it's there,
unfound,
waiting,
centuries late,
boiling,
swirling,
I've got the fix on
it,
it's coming into
focus,
don't you almost feel it
now?
I do.

barstool

the longer I live the more I realize
that I knew exactly what I was doing
when I didn't seem to be doing
anything
but watching a wet fly on the
bar
nuzzling a pool of
spilled beer.
I was quitting the game,
tossing in my hand
early,
it felt grand, I tell you,
it even felt dramatic, I mean
to cough it up and out,
to give way,
to sit there
the dirty Venetian blinds
behind me,
nothing to do but get my
wits up enough
to cage another free
drink.
I had zeroed out, I was
the Grand Marshal of
Nowhere,
still young,
I realized that there was
no place to go,
ever,
I was already there.
I was the Clown of the

Patrons.
I was the Nut.
I was the Heart of a
Heartless bar.

the drinks came.
the days and nights
went.
the years went.

I lived by my addled
crushed wits,
sometimes
ended up bloodied in
some alley, given up
for dead,
only to rise again.

I knew exactly what I
was doing: I was
doing nothing.
because I knew there
was nothing
to do.

I know now
that I knew then all that there
was to
know,
and tonight
sitting alone here,
nobody about,
I am still fixed in this
floating
perfect
aspect.

my wits have gotten me
from nowhere to
nowhere
and death like life
is lacking,
and I know so well
I did right
watching that fly
nuzzle the beer
suds
as the others
hustled their butts,
circled in the
tenebrous
light.

was Celine married?
did Hemingway have 6
cats?
why did Bogart smoke
himself to
death?
was Ty Cobb as mean
as they claim?
whatever happened to
Clark Gable's
ears?
did Van Gogh ever
ice skate?
where were you in
1929?
Nijinski was a
madman.
remember Admiral
Byrd?
Joe Louis was a
cobra.
remember a-dime-a-
dance?
Pearl Harbor?
Mutt and Jeff?
The Katzenjammer
Kids?
gluing together
balsa wood
airplanes?
a bagful

of candy for
7 cents?

remember the
iceman?
Slapsy Maxy
Rosenbloom?
garter belts?
garters?
all night movies?
marathon dance
contests?
Al Jolson?
Mickey Walker?
a nickel beer?
a nickel phone call?
a 3 cent stamp?
Primo Carnera?
a good ten cent
cigar?
Bull Durham?
fuse boxes?
ice boxes?
the ruler against
the open
palm?
the Indian head
penny?

Tom Mix?
Buck Rogers?
jaw breakers?
the WPA?
the NRA?
Jack Benny?
the Hit Parade?

movie houses with
ushers?
cigarettes called
Wings?

zoot suiters?
geeks?
grandmothers who
baked apple
pies?

gold-fish-eating
contests?
Red Grange?
the Babe holding
out for
80 grand?
Man of War?
flagpole-sitting
marathons?

I could go on
and on ...

but, Christ, if
you remember
all of these things
you must be
at least as old
as I am.

listing these things
on my
Macintosh
computer
with a 50-50 shot

of seeing the
21st
century,
betting the horse
instead of
riding it,
we're lucky to be
here and we'll
be lucky when we
leave.
see you in
St. Louis.
see you behind
that last curtain,
see you at another
time,
baby.

Paris

was just like not being there.

Celine was gone.

there was nobody there.

Paris was a bite of bluegrey air.
the women rushed by as if you would never
DARE to go to bed with
them.

there were no armies around.

everybody was rich.
there were no poor in view.
there were no old in view.

to sit at a table in a cafe
would get you careful stares from the other
patrons
who were certain that they were
more important than
you.
food was too expensive to eat.
a bottle of wine would cost you
your left hand.

Celine was gone.

the fat men smoked cigars and became
gloried puffs of smoke.

the thin men sat very straight and spoke
only to each other.
the waiters had big feet and were sure
that they were more important than
anything or
anybody.

Celine was gone.

and Picasso was dying.

Paris was absolutely nothing.

I did see a dog that looked like a
white wolf.

I don't remember leaving
Paris.

but I must have been
there.

it was somewhat like leaving
a fashion magazine in a
train station.

it's not enough that he's one of
the richest men on
television,
he has to reappear on the
tube
and complain that many other
programs are not
decent,
they are full of obscene
words and
gestures,
or that people are
"anti-social,"
that they should look up
to things that
will inspire
and purify
them.

his own program is
full of cute
children,
well-dressed, well-
fed,
overlooked by a
very understanding
father
and a mother
who understands the
father better than
he does

himself.
they live in a
luxurious home
and at times
certain members of
this family
have little
programmed arguments,
but they all work it
out,
become instruments
for a more
loving and understanding
togetherness.

all that I can say
to this
is:
shit, fuck, bullshit,
crap,
come here and
bite
this.

lousy mail

drinking up here, looking out at the lights of
the city, the rows of headlights snaking down
the Harbor Freeway south
forever,
Sibelius working on the radio.
there is a small refrigerator in the room.
I get up now, reach in there, crack a
beer as
Sibelius continues to work.

about 3 times a week now I get manuscripts
in the mail from young men
who seem to think that I can get them
published.
they tell me that their work is good.
I read it and find it astonishingly
bad.
they don't want to write, they want
fame.
they probably read their stuff to
their mothers, their girl
friends.
they probably give poetry readings
at poetry holes.
they will go on and on
typing dead work for decades
never believing that their failure is
simply the result of a lack of
talent.

as I sit tonight 3 such manuscripts
are on the desk in front of
me.
I don't know what to tell these
men.
they have no self-doubt.

I probably won't answer.

what would you tell them?

would you send them to hell
with a cruel comment?

would you give them
undeserved praise?

how can you be true and
kind at the same
time?

how?

THE SUICIDE

Contemplating suicide was standard practice for Marvin Denning. Sometimes his thinking about it disappeared for days, even for weeks, and he felt nearly normal, normal enough to continue living comfortably for a while. Then the urge would return. At those times life became too much for him, the hours and the days dragged along uselessly. The voices, the faces, the behavior of people sickened him.

Now, driving in from work the urge to suicide was fully there. He turned off the car radio. He had been listening to Beethoven's 3rd and the music had seemed all wrong, pretentious, forced.

"Shit," he said.

Marvin was driving over the bridge that took him back to his apartment. It was a bridge which spanned one of the largest harbors in the world.

Marvin stopped his car near the middle of the bridge, switched on the hazard light and got out of the machine. There was a ledge next to the bridge's rail and he stepped up on it.

Above him stretched a wire fence a good 10 feet tall. He'd have to climb that wire fence in order to get over the side.

Below him was the water. It looked peaceful. It looked just fine.

Rush hour traffic was building up. Marvin's car blocked the outer lane. The cars in that lane were trying to make a lane change. Traffic was backing up.

Some of the cars honked as they swung by. Drivers cursed Marvin as they drove by.

"Hey, you *nuts* or what?"

"Take a *dive*! The water's warm!"

Marvin continued to stare down at the water. He decided to climb the fencing and go over. Then he heard another voice.

"Sir, are you all right?"

A police car had parked behind Marvin's car. Red lights flashed. One officer approached him as the other remained in the car.

The officer moved quickly toward him. He was young with a thin white face.

"What's the problem, sir?"

"It's my car, officer, it has stalled, won't start."

"What are you doing up on the ledge?"

"Just looking."

"Looking at what?"

"The water."

The officer came closer.

"This is not a sightseeing area."

"I know. It's the car. I was just standing here, waiting."

Marvin stepped down from the ledge. The officer was next to him. He had a flashlight.

"Open your eyes wide, please!"

He shined the flashlight into Marvin's left eye, then his right, then he re-hooked the flashlight on his belt.

"Let me see your license."

The cop took the license.

"Stay where you are."

The cop walked back to the squad car. He stuck his head in the window and spoke with the other cop. Then he straightened up and waited. After a few minutes he walked back to Marvin, handed him back his license.

"Sir, we are going to have to move your car from the bridge."

"You mean you're going to call a tow truck? Thank you."

Marvin's car was parked on a slight incline near the center of the bridge.

"No, we are going to give you a push. Maybe when you get rolling you can get it started."

"That's very good of you, officer."

"Please get in your car, sir."

Marvin got in his car and waited. When the police car bumped his, he took off the hand brake and put it into neutral. They rolled up over the center of the bridge and down the other side. He put it into 2nd, stepped on the gas and, of course, the car started. He waved to the police and drove along.

They followed him. They followed him off the bridge and down the main boulevard. The blocks went by. They continued to follow. Then Marvin saw a cafe: The Blue Steer. He pulled into the parking lot, found a space.

The police car had pulled in behind him, a few yards to one side, between Marvin and the cafe. Marvin got out of his car, locked it and walked toward The Blue Steer. As he passed the cops in the squad car he gave them another little wave, "Thank you again, officers."

"Better get that car checked out, sir."

"I will, of course."

Marvin walked into the cafe without looking back. The restaurant was packed. All the faces almost made him sick. There was a sign:

PLEASE WAIT TO BE SEATED

Marvin didn't wait. He walked to the last empty booth, sat down. He wasn't hungry.

A huge waitress floated up in a pink outfit. She had a very round head and her lips were painted a bright raspberry. She handed him a shiny menu.

"How are you today?" she asked.

"Fine. And you?"

She didn't answer. Then she spoke.

"Coffee, sir?"

"No."

"Are you ready to order?"

"No. For the moment, bring me a glass of wine."

298

"What kind?"

"The house wine will do. Do you have port?"

The waitress left and he watched as her oversized buttocks worked away.

Maybe I can go back to the bridge tonight when there is nobody around, Marvin thought.

Two men had a table behind Marvin. He could hear them talking.

"The Dodgers are sure looking good, aren't they?"

"Yeah. And the Angels are right up there too. Just think of it. Maybe we can have a Freeway Series."

"That would be a hell of a hoot, wouldn't it?"

Then the waitress was back with Marvin's wine. She sat it down hard and some of the drink leaped out and splashed on the table.

"Sorry, sir."

"It's all right."

"Are you ready to order yet?"

"No, not yet."

"We have a sirloin steak special tonight."

"No, thank you."

Then she cranked up her buttocks and moved off. Marvin had a sip of the wine. It tasted dusty, somehow made him think of spiders. Then he heard the piped-in music. "*I don't have to say I love you,*" a male voice sang.

Then he heard the men behind him.

"I'm going to say something right now that you're not going to believe."

"Like what?"

"Ronald Reagan was the greatest president this nation ever had."

"Come on now, we've had a lot of them. That's a big statement."

"Without Reagan those fucking Russians would be all over the world, they'd be climbing over the fence and into our backyard. He stopped them where they should be stopped. They knew he meant business!"

299

"Well, yeah, he was a good man."

"I'll tell you something else. There's going to be a war in SPACE! Between the Russians and us! We're going to be fighting over the moon, over Mars, over all the planets!"

"We already got our flag on the moon."

Marvin finished his wine and got the attention of the waitress. She trundled over.

"Ready to order now, sir?"

"Another wine, please."

"We've got a sirloin steak special ..."

"Just the wine, please."

Marvin heard the piped-in music again. Another man was singing, he sang, "*If you don't answer the telephone soon, I'm gonna come to your room.*"

Then the waitress was back with his wine. She set it down.

"You see, I didn't spill it this time!"

She let loose an utterly false cackle of laughter.

"I'm getting better, you see?"

"You're all right ..."

"Diana's the name."

"You're all right, Diana."

Then she struggled off to her other duties. Evening had rapidly dissolved into night. Marvin sipped his wine.

When he hit that water it would be like hitting cement. Except he would slide into that blue cold—one leg like this, another like that—and the hair on his head floating out. Dumb shoes on dumb feet. Out of it. Zero minus zero. As ultimate as you could get, from here to nowhere. Fine enough. You couldn't have it all.

Suddenly there was a crash, the breaking of glass. The front door was kicked open and two men entered wearing stocking masks. A woman screamed.

"*Shut the fuck up or you're dead!*" the shorter man screamed. "*I mean it! No bullshit! Shape up or you're all dead!*"

Each man carried a canvas sack. The taller man moved to the cash register, hit a key, the drawer sprang open. He

300

began scooping bills and change into his sack.

Each man had what appeared to be a .357 Magnum.

"Don't anybody move!" yelled the shorter man.

He waved the Magnum over his head in a wild circle, then brought it down and pointed it around the cafe.

"O.K., all wallets and purses on the tables! Rings too! Watches! Everything! Anybody try any shit, it's your ass, got it?"

Then he began to move among the tables scooping everything into his sack.

The taller man was finished at the register. He saw the fat waitress cowering a few yards off. He ran up to her, said, *"Where's the money box?"*

"What?"

"The fucking money box! Where they keep the big bills!"

The fat waitress just stood there. The short man spun her around, jammed the Magnum against her neck.

"I'll blow your fucking head off! Where's the cash box?"

The fat waitress was sobbing, gulping for air. She said, *"It's in the kitchen! Under the sink!"*

"Don't anybody move!"

The tall man ran into the kitchen.

The short man pushed the frightened waitress to one side. He resumed clearing valuables off the tables, scooping them into his sack.

The tall man came running out of the kitchen.

"I got the fucking money! Let's go!"

The short man was busy.

"You watch the door! Nail anybody who comes in! Watch the door!"

"Come on, let's go, we got enough!"

"No, I'm going to get it all!"

He moved along until he got to Marvin's booth.

"Hey, fucker, where's your wallet?"

Marvin looked up at the stocking face. He rather liked it. The less you could see of the human face the more pleasant it was.

"I've decided to keep my wallet."

"You ain't deciding shit!"

"Of course I am."

"O.K., baby, you want it, you get it!"

Marvin felt the Magnum against his temple.

"Now, get out the wallet, O.K.?"

"Not O.K. I am keeping my wallet."

"Hey," yelled the tall man, *"let's get out of here!"*

The short man jammed the Magnum hard against Marvin's temple.

"You want this to be your last moment?"

"Go ahead and shoot," said Marvin.

Marvin waited. The safety catch went back on. Marvin saw the man switch his grip to the barrel of the Magnum. He saw the gun rise, sat there waiting. It smashed down on the top of his skull. There was an explosion of yellow, blue and red light but Marvin felt no pain. For a moment he couldn't move. Then he felt as if he could move. He tried it. He kicked out savagely and caught the man in the stomach with his right foot.

"Oooh ..."

The hold-up man dropped the sack, grabbed his groin, almost sank to one knee.

"Oh, God-damn it ..."

Marvin heard the safety catch go off again. The man aimed the Magnum, squeezed the trigger. The bullet whizzed past Marvin's left ear and broke an overhanging light fixture apart further down the room.

"Let's get out of here!" yelled the tall man.

The short man straightened up and walking half bent, and carrying his Magnum and his sack, he followed the tall man out the door. Then they were gone.

With that, the customers all started walking around and talking at once.

The cafe manager who had been hiding in the kitchen was on the telephone.

Marvin Denning finished his glass of wine and

motioned to the fat waitress who was standing just a few feet away, trembling. Marvin got up, walked over to her. "Diana, another glass of wine, please ..."

"Oh," she said, "oh ... yes ... of course ..."

Marvin went back and sat down. The noise of the patrons had risen to a sickening pitch as they talked about the hold-up.

Marvin waited, then Diana was back with his wine.

"Thank you, Diana."

He took a sip.

"That was a brave thing you did, sir. By doing that you saved the belongings of many of the customers."

"Oh ... yeah ..."

"You're *bleeding* poor man!"

"It's all right."

Diana ran off as well as she could. Denning heard the sound of the police siren. He took a napkin and held it up to the top of his head. Then he pulled it away and looked at it. Blood. The stupid simplicity of blood.

Then Diana was back.

"Here. All I could find was this dish towel but it's clean."

"Thanks."

He folded the towel and to please her he held it to the top of his head.

"You better get that sewed up."

"It's all right. Main thing: get me that steak you were talking about and maybe some french fries!"

Diana went back to the kitchen and Denning sipped his wine.

In another minute the police entered. They came running through the door, hands on holsters.

"Everybody stay where you are!"

One of the officers was the one with the thin white face, the same one who had stopped Denning on the bridge. Their eyes met. Thin white face stared at him.

"What're you doing here?"

"Waiting for a steak. You followed me over here, remember?"

Two more cops entered.

"Waiting for a steak?"

"Yes, any law against that?"

"Officer," said a patron who was standing nearby, "this is the man who almost captured one of the bandits. He kicked him to the floor."

Diana walked up with Denning's steak and fries, set it down.

"Officer, this is a very brave man," she said.

One of the patrons began to applaud. The others joined in.

Denning raised his wine glass to them, drained it.

Thin white face asked, "Did you know the hold-up men?"

"Can't say that I did."

Then Denning heard another siren. The patrons were pressing around his table.

The cop, irritated, said, "Stand back!"

A stocky, dumb-looking fellow in need of a shave came through the door followed by another cop. The stocky man pushed up to Denning's table.

"What's going on?"

"I've been held up, this place has been held up!" said the manager.

"Who are you?"

"Richard Fouts, manager of The Blue Steer."

The stocky man pulled out his badge. "Marsh Hutchinson, Hillside Division," he said.

Then he looked at Denning. Marsh took out his pen and pad.

"Who are you?"

"Marvin Denning, customer."

"He knocked one of those robbers right to the floor," said Diana.

"That right?" the stocky man asked Denning.

304

"Yeah, I kicked him in the balls."

"Why?"

"Is there a better place?"

"What'd he look like?"

"He looked like a man wearing a stocking mask."

"Height?"

"About 5-7."

"Weight?"

"Say, 145."

"Anything to distinguish him?"

"What do you mean?"

"What was the most outstanding feature you noticed?"

"He was carrying a .357 Magnum."

The stocky man inhaled, exhaled. "Denning, there's something I don't like about you."

"Hutchinson, we're even. There's something I don't like about you."

"O.K. You stay where you are."

He began questioning the manager of The Blue Steer.

Diana looked at Denning.

"Mind if I sit down? This whole thing has been too much for me."

"Sit down, sure."

Denning felt the whole booth give way as Diana put her buttocks down.

"You're brave," she said, "you're a brave man. I saw what you did."

"O.K." said Denning.

"I know this may shock you, and I know it will sound weird and crazy but ... I'd like to do something *nice* for you. Are you shocked?"

"No."

"Will you let me do something nice?"

"Sure."

"After all this is over we'll go to my place. Leave the steak. I'll cook you something better. Do you think I'm bold?"

"No."

"You know," Diana laughed, "when he put that gun to my head, I thought, I might die and I've ... I've never had a man. Isn't that terrible?"

"I guess it happens sometimes."

"I know I'm fat ... I'm embarrassed."

"It's all right."

"I should get you another wine."

"Why don't you?"

Diana struggled up and worked her way toward the kitchen.

Later, in the dark at Diana's place, he worked away. Denning hadn't worked so strenuously since he had been on a construction gang after high school and before college. Diana was groaning and moaning.

"Hold still, for Christ's sake!" he implored her.

Denning worked on, a good four minutes more, substituting fantasy after fantasy in his mind. Finally, he rolled off. He was in a sweat, inhaling and exhaling heavily. His head wound had broken open and he could feel a trickle of blood running down the back of his neck.

"Marvin," she said, "I love you."

"Thank you, Diana."

He got up and walked to the bathroom. He wetted a towel, cleaned off, then took the dry part of the towel and worked at the blood on his neck and head.

Well, many a man went to his death without having had a virgin. He wouldn't be one.

He threw the towel on the floor, walked out of the bathroom, through the bedroom and into the kitchen. He poured himself a glass of water at the sink and drank it down.

He looked around. Diana had a nice place. Maybe she got a lot of tips out of sympathy.

He found a can of beer in the refrigerator, cracked it, and sat at the breakfastnook table, sipping and smoking a cigarette he had found in a pack on the table. He finished the beer and the cigarette, walked back to the bedroom. Diana was in the bathroom. He began getting dressed. He heard her singing in the bathroom. Then the door opened and she walked out dressed in her nightwear. She saw him dressing and the happiness on her face vanished.

"Oh, you're leaving?"

"Yes."

"Will I see you again?"

"No."

"Oh, my God ..." She walked slowly over to the bed. She sat on the edge of the bed, her back to him. She just sat there, looking very large. The lights were out in the bedroom and just the light from the half-open bathroom door shone in.

Denning sat on a chair lacing his shoes.

The vision of the bridge now sat in the center of his brain, it beckoned, how it beckoned him once more. The water pulled at him as if it were a magnet.

Denning finished lacing his shoes, stood up.

"Goodbye, Diana."

She didn't answer. She just sat there. Denning could see little shivers running through her body. She was sobbing very quietly, trying to hold it back. It was almost obscene. Diana's head was bent forward. As Denning looked it seemed almost as if he were staring at the back of a large headless body.

"Listen," he asked after a long pause, "you got anything to eat around here?"

"What?"

"I asked if you had anything to eat around here."

She raised her head, turned.

"Oh. Oh yes, Marvin, I have a bottle of wine and a couple of steaks and some vegetables."

"Shall we have dinner?" Denning asked.

Diana rose from the bed as if she were weightless. It was very strange. Then she went off to the kitchen.

Denning took off his coat, sat back down in the chair,

took off his shoes, stockings, his pants and when she came back he was still in his shirt and shorts.

Diana walked through the doorway carrying a wine bottle, two glasses, the wine opener. She was having a little struggle carrying all that and she was laughing, not a loud laugh, but a continuous little joyous crazy laugh.

The light from the half-open bathroom framed her body, her face, the two glasses, the wine bottle, the wine opener.

Never before in the 46 years of his life had Marvin Denning seen a more beautiful woman.

confession of a genius

during world war two
some of the worst
writing of our time
appeared in books
and magazines,
it was truly
regrettable.
I lived
alone and
insane in tiny
rooms
being neither a
soldier nor a
writer.

it is possible to
be truly mad
and to still
exist
upon scraps
of
life.

I knew my
name,
was able to
dress myself,
was able to
speak the
language
but I was

entirely
inept,
without design,
I was a
meaningless
conglomeration
of
ideas.
I was an
idiot.

the army didn't
want me,
women didn't
want me
and I didn't want
myself.
I was a
husk.

yet twice
I found myself
with a typewriter.
I wrote a short
story which was
accepted by
a leading
magazine.
and I wrote
another which
appeared in an
intercontinental
journal
along with
Henry Miller
and

Camus.

then I hocked the
typewriter and
stopped
writing.
I felt that what I
had written was
meaningless.

I went from
city to city
from room to
room
from bar to
bar.

the war
ended and I
continued
existing in that
manner.

I read the
successful writers
and decided that
they too
were
meaningless.

I really didn't
begin writing
again
until I started
living with
women.
they startled

me
out of my
stupor,
dropped me
splashing and
thrashing into a
new
confusion.

my work began
to appear
in literary magazines.

people hated me
for the way
I wrote about
women.
but these people
never met the
women I
lived
with.
I was only
photographing
in words
the reality of
it all.

I wrote of my
horrible women
and my
horrible jobs
and the first damn
thing you knew
I had
half-a-fame.

I noticed that the
sycophants and
weaklings were
writing poetry.
so,
I tried that
too.
it was
easy.
the whole game
was just a matter
of tossing your
stuff at
them.

I gave readings,
packed them in,
I drank throughout,
insulting them,
tossing the
crap.
they hated it
and loved
it,
they ate up
my crap.

and through it
all
I had this
feeling of
bored
disinterest.

but then I
noticed that

the women I went
with were getting
younger,
with better bodies,
longer hair,
more light to their
eyes.

it was
paying off.
I no longer had to
hock typewriters
or work horrible
jobs.

I had become
something to
some
people.
others had
better sense.
but I was the
same
half-shot
asshole that
I had
always
been,
I was nothing
at all
but somehow
I had stumbled
into a lucky and
easy
game,
a shell game,

a hustle,
a lark,
a sunny
midnight,
a stance,
an
out,
an
in,
and yes I've been
there
ever
since.

traffic report

here in Los Angeles
on the freeways
it's like the Wild West
again.
many of the drivers carry guns
and if you cut them off
or irritate them in any manner
with your driving,
they simply pull up, point their
guns and begin
firing.
life has gotten to be too much
for many of us out
here,
the razor's edge is always
up
and any slight, slight as it might
be
becomes the ultimate and final
challenge.
many wait for it, many even hope
for it.
but out of it all, something else
has emerged:
far more polite driving habits.
who the hell wants to catch a
.32 caliber bullet in order to gain
3 car lengths in
heavy traffic?
me?
I'm so polite I'd make a nun

puke.
I prefer to die by my own
hand.

hands

I'm not even drinking
and I look down at my
hands and they look
large.
unfortunately for me
I've always had
small hands.

the hands are the
tools
for fist fights,
in gripping an
ax,
in strangling
and
related
exercises
I have always been
disadvantaged.

but now
my hands look
large.
I look down at
them
and they grow
larger.

they keep growing
it's
marvelous.

now I can
beat hell out of
some guy.

I decide to go
downstairs and
show my wife
my new
hands.

"look!" I'll say.
"look!"

and I'll hold
out my
hands.

and she'll say,
"what?
what is it?"

I decide not to
go downstairs.

I just sit here
and look at
my hands.

it is one of my
better
evenings.

yesterday I was
very
depressed.

at the track today
read where Kosinski
did it in the bathtub
with a bag over his
head.
bad health was
inferred
but loss of
stature and literary fame
are very unhealthy
to some.
plus New York
publisher's parties,
power plays,
and
the hint that
he had outside
help writing
his books.
he had friends
at *The New York
Times*,
enemies at the
Village Voice.
not killed by the
Holocaust,
he couldn't live
with the
critics.
bag over his
head

in a bathtub
full of
water.
what Hitler
couldn't do,
he did to
himself.
happy
journey.

the misanthrope

I've been accused of being
one.
well, I'm the ruins of Athens,
you know.
I'm always working to
rebuild, I'm on the
mend.

when I am with people
something gets subtracted
from me.
most people are hardly
joyous and seldom
interesting.
I listen to their complaints,
take note of their
braggadocio,
their unoriginal
insights.
they yawn my life
away.

you ask me to embrace
them?
I don't hate them,
I don't want to defeat
them or kill them.
I just want to get away
from them.

it is when I am alone

that I feel at my
best.
it is my normal
way,
it is when I smooth
out, float,
it is when whatever
light there is
enters
me.

the ruins of Athens.

the old bum.

the cockroach in the
cathedral.

the good wine.

the mental conversations
with Mrs. Death.

the dream of golden
windmills.

the inhaling of
life.

the soaring confinement.

the gentle walls.

if preferring this to
Humanity makes me a
misanthrope

then I
am

to the hilt,
gladly

now

here

tonight
tomorrow
next year

alone with
aloneness

finally.

putting it to bed

the first poem is the last poem is the
best poem
pulling its stockings off
late in the night of the
morning
the best poem is the last
poem
the poem poem poem
as nine tenths of the people of
this city are
asleep
I am up with the murderers and the
thieves and the cab drivers
and some of the
prostitutes
and many of the drunks
and the mad
and the insomniacs
and the etc.
I murder the language
I steal the language,
I drink the language,
I am mad with the language
in the cab of my mind,
I am a whore.

the last poem
running out of my fingers

soon I will be asleep with
my wife and my
cats.

we will be all in the same
room,
still,
except for some wheezings
and turnings
and this last poem will
sit in this room
and I will be in the other
room
and some day you will
read this poem,
perhaps,
and think,
that guy makes too much
of it.

the last poem
the last poem
the best for me.

the trash can

this is great, I just wrote two
poems I didn't like.

there is a trash can on this
computer.
I just moved the poems
over
and dropped them into
the trash can.

they're gone forever, no
paper, no sound, no
fury, no placenta
and then
just a clean screen
awaits you.

it's always better
to reject yourself before
the editors do.

especially on a rainy
night like this with
bad music on the radio.

and now—
I know what you're
thinking:
maybe he should have
trashed this
misbegotten one

also.

ha, ha, ha,
ha.

block

in the past two months the poems have
riveted themselves to paper in ungodly
numbers
and if a poet may judge—
most of them were of high quality.
now I have become spoiled,
I walked into here tonight expecting
more luck
but the night has been slow.
and rightfully so—
occurrence must precede action,
the tank must refill.
writing, at its best, is not a contest,
it's not even an occupation,
it's a hazardous madness
that arrives at its own
behest.
prod it and you lose it.
pretend, and the words fall
ill.

when the lulls arrive there is
nothing to do but
wait,
do other things.

the writing must leap upon you
like a wild beast.

there are none of those in this
room with me

tonight.
they are elsewhere.
they are with somebody
else.

so all I can do is sit in this chair
tonight
and tell you that I can't
write.

there are other things to do.
like now I am going downstairs
to see my wife
and my 6 cats
and they will see me
and we will look at each
other.
it will be all right.
I'm sure it
will.

they might even remember
me.

storm

a storm at last in this damned Los Angeles
desert,
even the lights went out in the neighborhood,
most of the people asleep,
the drunks just pour another drink,
I poured another drink,
1:42 a.m.
the lights go back on,
Brahms begins to play on the radio again,
I think of Turgenev, just for the hell of it,
just because I like his name.
there are good names: Mozart, Celine,
Artaud, Bach.
some names ring through and stick.
anyhow, it's raining and raining and raining.
and Joe Louis is dead and Ty Cobb is dead
and it's been a long time since the Waner brothers
patrolled the outfield in Pittsburgh
and whatever happened to Smith Brothers cough
drops?
I used to eat them like candy.
we need the rain.
we need the rain.
we need it.
I used to eat those cough drops like candy and I had
a dot-and-dash set and I knew the Morse code and I
sent out S.O.S.s for years but help never
came.

Turgenev.
I wish my name was Turgenev.

hello, I am Ivan Turgenev and it's raining and I'm writing
about the rain
it rains hard here in Russia and the nights are black and
the days are black
and my girlfriend keeps telling me about our leader who has
arching eyebrows.
and I say, "oh, yes, very interesting ..."
my name is Turgenev and it's raining and we need the
rain.

ran into Gorky the other day and he said rain was just so
much capitalist bullshit.
crazy guy, crazy.

well, it's 1:58 a.m. and I am sleepy.

sleeping in the rain helps me forget things like I am going
to
die and you are going to die and the cats are going to die
but it's still good to stretch out and know you have arms
and
feet and a head, hands, all the parts, even eyes to close
once
more, it really helps to know these things, to know your
advantages
and your limitations, but why do the cats have to die, I
think that the
world should be full of cats and full of rain, that's all, just
cats and
rain, rain and cats, very nice, good
night.

the similarity

lost another 3 page poem to this computer,
reminds me of the past,
you know, with some women
you leave them in bed
before going off to the warehouse
to work
and you ask them,
"Baby, you going to be here when I
get back?"
"sure, Hank, I love you ..."

and you come back to find the bed cover
flipped back, they slipped out right after
you drove off,
didn't even empty an
ashtray.

well, you're a fool but you don't give up
on women on account of
that.

the next one might be
better.

and this poem can't replace the one
lost
but it's a good shot in the dark
which beats
none at
all

maybe.

My Madness

There are degrees of madness, and the madder you are the more obvious it will be to other people. Most of my life I have hidden my madness within myself but it is there. For instance, some person will be speaking to me of this or that and while this person is boring me with their stale generalities, I will imagine this person with his or her head resting on the block of the guillotine, or I will imagine them in a huge frying pan, frying away, as they look at me with their frightened eyes. In actual situations such as these, I would most probably attempt a rescue, but while they are speaking to me I can't help imagining them thus. Or, in a milder mood, I might envision them on a bicycle riding swiftly away from me. I simply have problems with human beings. Animals, I love. They do not lie and seldom attempt to attack you. At times they may be crafty but this is allowable. Why?

Most of my young and middle-aged life was spent in tiny rooms, huddled there, staring at the walls, the torn shades, the knobs on dresser drawers. I was aware of the female and desired her but I didn't want to jump through all the hoops to get to her. I was aware of money, but again, like with the female, I didn't want to do the things needed to get it. All I wanted was enough for a room and for something to drink. I drank alone, usually on the bed, with all the shades pulled. At times I went to the bars to check out the species but the species remained the same—not much and often far less than that.

In all the cities, I checked out the libraries. Book after book. Few of the books said anything to me. They were mostly dust in my mouth, sand in my mind. None of it related to me or how I felt: where I was—nowhere—what I had—nothing—and what I wanted—nothing. The books of the centuries only compounded the mystery of having a name, a body, walking around, talking, doing things. Nobody seemed stuck with my particular madness.

In some of the bars I became violent, there were alley fights, many of which I lost. But I wasn't fighting anybody in particular, I wasn't angry, I just couldn't understand people, what they were, what they did, how they looked. I was in and out of jail, I was evicted from my rooms. I slept on park benches, in graveyards. I was confused but I wasn't unhappy. I wasn't vicious. I just couldn't make anything out of what there was. My violence was against the obvious trap, I was screaming and they didn't understand. And even in the most violent fights I would look at my opponent and think, why is he angry? He wants to kill me. Then I'd have to throw punches to get the beast off me. People have no sense of humor, they are so fucking serious about themselves.

Somewhere along the way, and I have no idea where it came from, I got to thinking, maybe I should be a writer. Maybe I can put down the words that I haven't read, maybe by doing that I can get this tiger off my back. And so I started and decades rolled by without much luck. Now I was a mad writer. More rooms, more cities. I sunk lower and lower. Freezing one time in Atlanta in a tar paper shack, living on one dollar and a quarter a week. No plumbing, no light, no heat. I sat freezing in my California shirt. One morning I found a small pencil stub and I began writing poems in the margins of old newspapers on the floor.

Finally, at the age of 40, my first book appeared, a small chapbook of poems, *Flower, Fist and Bestial Wail*. The package of books had arrived in the mail and I opened the package and here were the little chapbooks. They spilled on the sidewalk, all the little books and I knelt down among them, I was on my knees and I picked up a *Flower Fist* and I kissed it. That was 30 years ago.

I'm still writing. In the first four months this year I have written 250 poems. I still feel the madness rushing through me, but I still haven't gotten the word down the way I want it, the tiger is still on my back. I will die with that son-of-a-bitch on my back but I've given him a fight. And if there is anybody out there who feels crazy enough to want to become a writer, I'd say go ahead, spit in the eye of the sun, hit those keys, it's the best madness going, the centuries need help, the species cry for light and gamble and laughter. Give it to them. There are enough words for all of us.

pastoral

listening to a piano and a
trumpet
mix it up
on the radio,
the express purpose of
existence remains
unsolved.
all 6 cats are asleep
now,
12:30 a.m.,
my wife is across the
street visiting with a
neighbor lady.
good, they need
it.
the racetrack was
closed today
and I was a lost
fat
butterfly.
most days go
nowhere
but the avoidance
of pain and
dissolution are
lovely.
they will arrive
soon enough,
fecund,
recharged,
valiant,

evermost.

now there is a
chorus on the radio,
they sing to me
as I clean my
fingernails with a
toothpick.

no thunder
tonight.
no tiger roaring
in my brain.

I am resting.
I rub my face with
my fingers.

I am waiting for
war.
the centuries have
trained me
well.

I lean back in the
chair
and smile
to myself,
for myself,
for everything,
for nothing.
this is absolutely
great.
this is as good as
it is ever
going to
get.

those times are gone now
but I remember the 50s
at the track, people crushed
around the bars, laughing,
wise cracking and there were
fist fights, there were crowds
of 50 and 60 thousand people
on the weekends, it seemed
everybody had money and
even the mutuel clerks were
happy; good-looking prosti-
tutes were everywhere and
Willie Shoemaker was young,
even Johnny Longden was
young and Ralph Neves
smoked cigarettes in the
walking ring, you saw George
Raft, and there were 8 races
instead of 9 and there was
the feeling that you were
going to make money and if
you didn't, what the hell,
they were running the next
day.
and there was always a
woman with you and if there
wasn't there would be
that night.

it was gamble and drink
and forget

tomorrow.

those were the 50s.

go out there now, it's sparse
and drab, it's like a home for
the mentally deficient.
nobody's laughing,
the rent money's up
for grabs and
the ladies are old, white-
haired, they sit together,
bet two dollars to
show.
they are terrified of
everything.
they should be.

the bartenders have
nothing to do.

the track gives away
prizes, trinkets
trying to draw the
crowds.
the track offers
exotic betting.
the crowd does not
arrive
and what there is
begins leaving
after each race.
there are now 9 races,
it doesn't matter—
there is no money to
bet,

the track is a funeral
parlor, it is the end
of life.
the sun can't make it
through the filthy
air.
it gets dark soon.

the people move
slowly toward the
exits.
their faces are
unhappy, their faces
are
murdered.
it is a procession of
the dead.

it's the 90s.

it's 40 years back to the
50s,
it's centuries back.

it's the 90s.

nobody's laughing.

tomorrow is all too
close.

the last race is here.

that rare good moment

when the gods relent
when the dogs back
off,
you are sitting in a
Sushi joint
working the chopsticks
between two tall bottles of
Kirin
and you are quietly thinking
about any number of Hells
you have
survived,
probably no more than
anybody else
but they're yours to
remember.
survival is a very
funny thing,
and it's weird,
passing safely through all the
wars,
the women,
the hospitals, the jails,
youth,
middle-age,
suicide dances,
decades of
nothingness.

now in a Sushi joint
on a side street

in a small town,
it all passes before
you
quickly
like a bad/good
movie.

there is this
strange feeling of
peace.

not a car passing
in the street,
not a sound.

you hold the chopsticks
as if you have used
them for
centuries,
note a tiny piece of
coleslaw at the
edge of your
plate.
there, you have it,
all that style,
grace,
god damn it's so
strange
to feel good to
be alive,
doing nothing
exceptional
and feeling
the glory of
that,
like a full

choir behind
you,
like the
sidewalks,
like the
doorknobs.

grass grows in Greece
and even ducks
sleep.

doesn't seem like much

my editor-publisher who is about
60
writes me,
"let's go another ten years.
you up to it?"
I'm 70.

ten years?
that's just a walk around the
block.
I feel almost
insulted.
how about 30
years?
a man can get a little
work done in that
time.

I don't answer my editor-
publisher.
is he getting
tired?
what else would he do
if he wasn't publishing
me?
work his garden?
play golf?
travel?

well, in a sense I *do*
answer him

by sitting down to the
keyboard
and typing out
poems
in different type faces,
on different
colored papers,
just to pep up the
show,
and the content is
good too—ripely
burning and also
laughing a
bit.

ten years?
this is 1991.
the year 2,000 will
come and go
in the blink of an
eye.

hey, editor-publisher,
how about the year
2020?

then we can putter in
our gardens and write
our goddamned auto-
biographies.

you up to it?

strange luck

slapped across the face with a
shit brick
he stopped at Biff's Bar
for a quick one and stayed
five years.
he survived through and with
a half-witted
guile.
he was evicted from room after
room.
within a four block area he
had lived in nine
rooms.
each was about the same:
dirty, small, gloomy.
he lived on loaves of bread
alone.
at rare times he added
bologna or peanut
butter.
in the bar it was beer,
beer, beer
and at rare times,
whiskey or vodka or
scotch or gin.
gin didn't do much for
him but he
welcomed it.

nobody knew where he had
come from, what he wanted.

the others accepted him
as a fixture, an oddball
fixture.
the women, largely, ignored
him.

he was neither bitter, angry
or displeased
he was just there.

then, one day, after 5 years
he just walked out and was
never seen there
again.

now he owns a large home, a
late model car,
there is a spa, a swimming
pool, a vast garden, a
wife.
sometimes you will read of
him in the
metropolitan
dailies.

he still drinks,
but moderately.
beer, wine or an occasional
vodka.

he drinks alone
in an upstairs room.
he sits at the keyboard of an
expensive
computer.

those few who remember him
can't believe the
transition.

he knows that is all
just game-playing by the
gods.

he feels no different than
he ever
did.
he is no less or no more
than he was
then.

he drinks at the computer
and waits for death
as he has always
done.

it's hard but it's
fair.

and strange and strange and
strange and
strange.

until it hurts

you have to wait until it
hurts, until it clangs in
your ears like the bells
of hell, until nothing
else counts but it, until
it is everything,
until you can't do any-
thing else
but.

then sit down and write
or stand up and
write
but write
no matter what
the other people are
doing,
no matter what
they will do to
you.

lay the line down,
a party of one,
what a party,
swarmed by the
light,
the time of the
times,
out of the tips of
your
fingers.

DEATH IN THE AFTERNOON

We are in Musso's Restaurant around 2 p.m., it's the best time there, the tablecloths aren't on the dinner tables yet and it's quiet. The tourists are all at Disneyland. I'm having a turkey sandwich with a side order of fries. I don't know what Blackwell is eating. It's a large rectangle of meat very well done (almost black) but inside it's a bright red. He slices very thin portions and chews each piece with great reverence. Outside, Hollywood Boulevard has disintegrated into skid row. Just Musso's stands there as it has since 1919, the last bit of class in sight. It is a good place to be when you are feeling down and I am usually feeling down.

"Well, what ya gonna do?" Blackwell asks me.

"Do? I'll just get rid of the girl. I'm too old now to take any more gorings. I feel like an old matador who wants to hang it up."

"You've lived with a dozen women in the last 15 years. How ya gonna break the habit?"

"How can you eat that raw meat?" I ask Blackwell. "Don't you feel as if you're eating something alive?"

"Better that than the other way around."

"Pardon me, I've got to piss. Order me another beer, will you?"

I get up and walk toward the rear. There is Fellini leaning against the wall. Not *that* Fellini. This one is a waiter. Whenever Fellini sees me he unfurls this great big smile but it's almost always as if he was laughing at me.

"How are the ponies going, buddy?" he asks me.

"Night harness racing right now ..."

"I know, but there is also the thoroughbreds down at Del Mar. I was there last Sunday. Didn't make much. $280. Had my wife along. She spoiled my concentration."

Fellini always wins, he says.

I go in to piss, I do, then wash my claws, come out. Fellini is still standing there. Still smiling like a blazing sunset.

I stop.

"Reminds me," I tell him. "Damndest thing happened at the harness races the other night. Got a lot of things on my mind, you know. For example, I got these 3 creatures in my front hedge, large as cats. They come out every night and raid my vegetable garden. Anyhow, it's the last race, I'm a few bucks in the hole, maybe 5, and I decide to go $50 win, and besides being distracted by the hookers with no panties on, I get a toothache. I'm also trying to get the late action, I'm watching my horse, and at the last flash my horse drops from 5/2 to two-to-one and I run up to the window and bet $50 win."

"What happens?" Fellini asks, still smiling.

"What *happens*? I look down at my ticket later and I realize I'm really *fucked*!"

"Oh yeah?" he smiles.

"Yeah. I had gone up and hollered out, 'Fifty-to-win on the 2!' I had been thinking *odds*, you know what I mean? I had mistakenly bet on the *two horse* and he was reading *fifty-to-one on the board*!"

"A guy will always find a way to lose," smiles Fellini.

"Only," I say, "the 2 gets up in the last jump and pays $108.40. I get back $2,710.00."

Fellini's face darkens. The smile jumps from that physiognomy, runs into the men's room and slithers down the nearest latrine.

I walk back to the table feeling good, sit down and Blackwell is still slicing at his red death lunch. I take a pull of beer.

"The old matador returns," chews Blackwell.

"What?"

"You called yourself the old matador, said you didn't want to be gored anymore."

352

"Don't worry. I'll get rid of her. Just finish your kill."

"Reminds me," he says, "I had a horrible hangover the other morning. Been drinking red wine and scotch. I can't get out of bed. I kick on the tv. And there's one of those old movies they've shown over and over. Anyhow, I watched. It was about an old matador ..."

"Uh ..."

"I watch, and the way I get it, the old matador had been or was, the greatest."

"Huh ..."

Then Blackwell looks at me, "Aren't you gonna finish your turkey sandwich?"

"Not today ..."

"Can I have it?"

I shove the sandwich toward him.

"How about the fries?" he asks.

"No, I'm keeping my fries."

"Oh," says Blackwell. "... Anyhow, where I come in on this film the old matador is very upset. He's in his dressing room, sitting in front of the mirror, arranging himself, getting ready, you know. His handlers are running around like sissies. Suddenly the old matador rips off his fake pigtail and throws it to the floor. 'What the hell's the matter?' one of his handlers asks him."

Blackwell stops. "Hey, listen, buddy, isn't that Jonathan Winters over there, sitting at that table?"

I look: "Yes, it is ... Don't stare. He's been in the funny farm, you know. Don't stare. Let him eat in peace."

Blackwell sighs, "Well, anyhow the old matador says, '*I'm not going on!*' 'What? What? What?' the 3 or 4 handlers ask. '*I'm getting out of here!*' the old matador screams. He knocks down his handlers and runs out the door."

I look up. It's Fellini. He's still not smiling. He looks at me: "I don't believe that story you told me about the 50-to-one shot."

"Are you our waiter?" I ask him.

"No."

"Then, will you please inform *our* waiter that I wish another beer and that my friend here would like a glass of Corvo Salaparuta White, and if you don't have that, then please, the *nearest* thing ..."

Fellini walks off to find Swanney, our waiter. Swanney is a real nice fellow, he's always consoling me about those animals in my front hedge who eat the red cabbage, the carrots, the zucchini and the eggplant.

"Where was I?" asks Blackwell.

"The way I see it, the old matador has decked a few of his boys and is running out the door ..."

"Oh, yeah, he has decided not to fight at the arena that day with the rising young matador on the same card. There's been so much *said* about the young matador, and on top of that the old matador had just recently seen his best friend killed in the ring, another *old* matador ..."

"You must have been really sick to keep watching that movie."

"Yeah. Mixing the drinks like that."

"Here come our drinks. Good old Swanney!"

He puts down the drinks, looks at me. "Are those animals still eating your celery stalks?"

"Yes, Swanney. I am considering Capital Punishment."

"Anything else, sir?"

"Isn't that enough?"

"All right," continues Blackwell, "the old matador leaps into his car and drives away, but guess what?"

"What?"

"He's followed by ... Jonathan Winters is *leaving*."

"We all must, at some time, do that."

"You're right. Anyhow, the old matador is being followed by this lovely rich redhead. They met casually one time down by the bull stables, the rich redhead turning it on and the old matador hardly noticing. I mean, why should he? Don't those guys get a gift of a virgin after every great performance?"

"Here," I say, "take my fries ..."

354

"Oh. All right. So, the rich redhead follows him. Her car is faster. The old matador can't elude her. He stops his car. He gets out. 'Why are you following me?' he asks."

Fellini is back. "Listen," he says to me, "I wasn't meaning to be impolite. What I was inferring was that maybe we both exaggerate about the horses ..."

"Fellini," I say, "show me a horseplayer who doesn't and I'll show you a liar ..."

Fellini leaves.

"So," says Blackwell, "she switches on her car radio while the old matador is standing there and he *hears* the mob at the arena, they are going crazy with sorrow and anger because the old matador has run off ..."

"He rushes back to the arena?" I suggest.

"No. She looks at him. She says, 'We need to talk. Follow me!' And then she leaps into her sports car, spins it around in the dirt road as he watches her. Then he leaps into his car and follows ..."

I flag Swanney for refills as Blackwell consumes my last fry and continues. "They get to her place, a mansion. They walk through the mansion and go out to a garden patio, sit at a table. The servant arrives with refreshments."

"Now," I suggest, "they will begin to commiserate with each other about his tormented soul and that commiseration will lead to further torment ..."

"Do you think *everybody* has bad luck with women like you do?"

After that we fall into 4 minutes of silence. Swanney comes with more drinks and Blackwell orders a plate of fries. He looks at me. "Eating is better than fucking, it takes longer and you can do it more often."

"Do tell me more about the old matador ..."

"O.K. They are in the patio and the old matador looks around. 'You own all this?' he asks. The redhead nods in the affirmative. He explains, 'I admire wealth.' "

"That's when you turn the set off?"

"Right. I get up, puke. Then I mix half a bottle of beer

355

with the same amount of tomato juice, sprinkle in a touch of paprika and ground pepper, drink some and switch the set back on ..."

"They're drunk?" I ask, "and she's holding a red table-cloth and he's charging it like a bull?"

"No, there's been a passage of time. The old matador has been living there 3 or 4 days when his new rival, the young matador, arrives. The rich redhead asks the young matador what he wants. 'I know that he is here, Senora!' he replies. And he goes on to make a speech about how he has worshipped the old matador since he was a boy and he has dreamed of fighting on the same card with him ..."

"How *terribly* dull. Can I have one of your french fries when they arrive?" I ask.

"Sure ..."

"The young matador and the rich redhead stare at each other. Then the young matador says, 'I must go!' He seems to be a dull fellow but I guess all you need to be a bullfighter is a lack of imagination and good reflexes ..."

"Oh," I say, "please tell me what happens next!"

"Sure. Before the young matador can leave the old matador steps up and tells the redhead, 'I must go back!' "

"It is a great moment," I say.

We fall into another 4 minutes of reflective silence. The skid row of Hollywood Boulevard bakes in the sun outside as we sit lost in the heart of Mexico. The fries arrive. Blackwell passes the plate. I spear the biggest, fattest, yellowest of them all, bite off a hot end as Blackwell continues.

"So, of course, the next scene we are there. The bull ring. The young matador goes on first. He makes glorious and impossible movements as the bull charges—such innovative classicism. Again and again. And then—the perfect kill."

"One more fry and I won't bug you anymore."

Blackwell passes the plate. "Say, wasn't that Allen Ginsberg who just walked in?"

"No, that was Andy Warhol."

356

"Well," says Blackwell, "next scene. On walks the old matador to a chorus of boos, pure hatred."

"Is there any other kind?" I ask.

"Hell, I don't know. Anyhow, the old matador just stands there. He looks pitiful like he can't get off the dime. His buttocks are all bunched up and quivering ..."

"On a woman that wouldn't be bad."

"I know," says Blackwell. "Anyhow, the old matador draws the meanest bull of them all: 'Muerto.' "

I flag Swanney for a new set of drinks. (When I want to get a waiter's attention I always wrap a napkin around a fork and wave. When I am with the ladies it always disgusts them, but waiters respond when they see it.)

"Anyhow," continues Blackwell, "the old matador draws Muerto but the picadors screw up the banderilla job— very sloppy about it. When Muerto makes his first charge at the old matador, the picadors hardly touch him as Muerto rushes past the old matador, who almost fertilizes his shorts."

"No shit?"

"The old matador shakes the cape through the laughter of the crowd and Muerto charges again. This time the old matador is a bit more graceful."

"Ah ..."

"Yes. The crowd grows quiet. As Muerto moves in again the old matador seems to find his legs, his youth, his courage ... he executes a perfect *Digaxxello!*"

"A *what?*"

"Forgive me. It's been 40 years since I've read Barnaby Conrad or Hemingway ..."

"Do you know that Faulkner used to drink here at Musso's?"

"Yeah, anyhow, the old matador has Muerto charmed. Muerto moves in again to be baffled by the soundless *Tearasouloh* ..."

"As the crowd roars?"

"... wildly, remembering the old matador at his best,

but *never* ... like *this*! The massive and beautiful bull, an instrument of the old matador's will ..."

"Andy Warhol just left," I say. "I think we've been here a long time too ..."

"He's probably going back to New York," says Blackwell.

"I hope," I say, "so."

"Anyhow," says Blackwell, "there are more brave and symphonic moves by the old matador. Now, Muerto the magnificent bull is helpless. The time for the kill has come."

"And here," I say, "come our drinks."

They are set down before us. We nod, pick up our drinks, click a toast in the Spanish manner.

"... Up high in the stands, sitting in a box with the President of Mexico, the rich redhead's eyes glisten with love for the old matador."

"He know where she sits?"

"Yes. And in the midst of a *Figeralla* he looks up and catches her eye, smiles, waves, and that's all the opportunity Muerto needs. He gets the left horn in, guts the matador, lifts him high, shakes him like a sawdust doll, shows him to the sun ..."

"Shit ..."

"But he's not quite dead. Don't you go to the movies?"

"Mostly just to eat popcorn in the dark."

"Well, the next scene is in the infirmary. The old matador is stretched there on a table with many people milling around. The old matador raises his hand and gestures for them to leave ... and they do ... and he's left alone with the redhead. She looks into his eyes. She says, 'You were beautiful!' "

"The old matador," I ask, "smiles?"

"Yes, and she kisses him on the mouth, hard. Then she straightens and looks sadly down at him as the people file back in."

"Great timing."

"She turns, tells them, 'The matador is dead ...' "

358

"You know," I tell Blackwell, "when I'm in a real depressed mood—which is most of the time—it's always great to listen to you tell some long story which fails to make me laugh."

"I'm sorry. Maybe we can try again sometime?"

"Sure. But what was it you wanted to see me about today?"

"Hey," says Blackwell, "I thought you wanted to see *me* ..."

Out in the parking lot I can't quite find my car. I've lost my parking ticket. I feel like the old matador, I am surely much older than the old matador.

I find my car, get in. It starts.

The sun is going down.

I drive out of there more depressed and alienated than ever. The beautiful people are useless and everybody else is dull.

I cut south on Cherokee, wait at the red light as some dried-up, worked-over, unimaginative 8 or 9 helpless citizens walk this way and that. I get the green light, move through the warm evening, get onto the freeway where I immediately incite a challenge from 3 kids in a souped-up Chevy. So I step on it, and here they come after me, leering, giving me the finger, as a shitty afternoon turns into a shitty evening. I luck out. They run into a traffic jam. I find the free lane inside, jump up to 85, 90, then check the rearview mirror, see them caught back there, and I am in San Pedro.

I find my place, pull into the driveway, park it, get out, just another old matador. But inside, as I open the door, my favorite white cat, The Jinx, leaps up into my arms and suddenly I am in love again.

the gods

I sit here on the 2nd floor
hunched over in yellow
pajamas
still pretending to be
a writer.
some damned gall,
at 71,
my brain cells eaten
away by
life.
rows of books
behind me,
I scratch my thinning
hair
and search for the
word.

for decades now
I have infuriated the
ladies,
the critics,
the university
suck-toads.

they all will soon have
their time to
celebrate.

"terribly overrated …"

"gross …"

"an aberration ..."

my hands sink into the
keyboard
of my
Macintosh,
it's the same old
con
that scraped me
off the streets and
park benches,
the same simple
line
I learned in those
cheap rooms,
I can't let
go,
sitting here
on this 2nd floor
hunched over in yellow
pajamas
still pretending to be
a writer.

the gods smile down,
the gods smile down,
the gods smile down.

sitting, talking through the
night, it's a
malfeasance trying to
feel good, the empty
beer and wine bottles
gathering, the ashtrays
runneth over,
twice-told jokes are
told again,
somebody's religiosity
is hurt,
politics limp in and out,
death comes in with heavy
shoes and kicks holes in
the air,
somebody complains of
bad luck,
forgotten movies are
discussed that would
rather have remained
forgotten.
nobody talks of books,
of paintings,
of the stock market or
the life of the
inch worm.

each person quietly
mocks the other person,
in a wholesome, good-
natured way

(of course).
some heads fall,
others
laugh.

it is an evening of
friends and
relatives.

the hours inch-worm
along.

they and we are in the
trenches
of hell,
throwing mud at the
fates.

then they grow weary of
the absurd battle and
leave
one by
one.

then there is just the
wife and
myself.

soon she goes up the
stairway
and I am left with
myself,
right back where I
began.

I sit there

lighting
cigars.

there are still things
to be
resolved
but what are
they?

I turn out the lights
and sit in the
dark.
then I see a strange headless
thing walk up to the
glass door.
it places its paws
high
upon the
door and
leans there.
its eyes are in its
belly.
one is gold and
glowing.
the other is green
with shots of
red.

I walk up the stairway,
climb into
bed.
my wife snores
peacefully.

the night is finished.
I am still alive.

the bluebird swallows
the worm.
the harbor tangles with
the fog.
morning swarms the
window.
I am a joke told
again.

I sleep.

a great show

when I went to visit my friend
at the Motion Picture Hospital,
it was full of actors and
freaks and directors and
assistant directors and grips
and cameramen and film editors
and script writers and sound
men and etc.
some of them were sick
some of them were dying
but somehow it wasn't like a
regular hospital,
that special heavy darkness
wasn't there,
everything was:
"LIGHTS! CAMERA! ACTION!"
everybody still
on the
set.
at least, it seemed like that
to me.
as bad as most Hollywood
movies had been, were and
still are,
there remained the touch of
the brave and dramatic in
the air.

when I went to the cafeteria,
everything was on cue:
even the people in wheelchairs made

dramatic gestures, spoke in
senatorial tones; they had
fierce blue eyes,
white, carefully cropped
beards,
deliberate enunciations,
there was blithe bullshit,
a whole Shakespearean
afterglow.

dwarfs sitting at tables
eating blueberry
pie.
old script writers, all
looking Faulknerian
musing about their drunken
afternoons at Musso and
Frank's.
old dolls, once beautiful
now toothlessly munching
soft toast, poking at
peaches.

and almost all the rooms
were private,
arranged to bring in the
light of hope.
the nurses, as in all
hospitals
worked their asses
off,
and the doctors were
congenial,
good actors in a bad
scene.

and my friend, who was
dying, spoke to me
not of his death
but of his idea for
his next
novel.

he also spoke of the
crazies and geniuses
or would-be
geniuses
running
loose.

"we've got one of the
original Tarzans here,"
he told me.
"every now and then he
runs all over the
place
giving his Tarzan
yodel and looking for
his Jane."

"they let him run
loose?"

"oh, yes, he doesn't
harm anybody.
we rather like it."

well, my friend
died, so I didn't go
there anymore.

but it was a very odd
visitation.

death was there but
death was on camera
as He was so often in
Hollywood.
it was as if
everybody was ready for
the last scene,
having practiced it so
often
already.

and about a month
later
I read a small bit in
the paper:
Tarzan had
died,
perhaps he has gone
on to find his
Jane.

there are still happy
endings, aren't
there?

like my friend who
died
his books have become
famous throughout much
of the
world.

which is only half a
happy ending
but at least his widow
in Malibu

won't have to baby
sit
to have bacon with
her
eggs.

epilogue

Fante gone to Hollywood,
Fante on the golf course,
Fante at the gambling tables,
Fante in a home in Malibu,
Fante a friend of William
Saroyan.
But Fante, I remember you
best,
in the 1930s
living in that hotel next to
Angel's Flight,
struggling to be a writer,
sending stories and letters
to Mencken.
the scream came from
the gut
then.
I heard it.
I still hear it.
and I refuse to imagine you
on a golf course
or in Hollywood.

but now it doesn't matter.
you're dead
but the good writing
remains
and the way you helped
me get the line down
the way I
wanted it.

I'm glad I finally met you
even though you were
dying
and remember when I
asked you,
"listen, John, whatever
happened to that
Mexican girl in
Ask the Dust?"

and you answered,
"she turned out to be
a goddamned
lesbian!"

and then the nurse
came in with your
big white
pill.

every now and then it comes back to
me,
him in bed there, blind,
being slowly chopped away,
the little bulldog.
the nurses passing through, pulling
at curtains, blinds, sheets.
seeing if he was still alive.
the Colorado Kid.
the scourge of the *American
Mercury*.
Mencken's Catholic bad boy.
gone Hollywood.
and tossed up on shore.
being chopped away.
chop, chop, chop.
until he was gone.

he never knew he would be
famous.
I wonder if he would have given
a damn.
I think he would have.

John, you're big time now.
you've entered the Books of
Forever
right there with Dostoevsky,
Tolstoy, and your boy
Sherwood Anderson.

I told you.

and you said, "you wouldn't
shit an old blind man,
would you?"

ah, no need for that,
bulldog.

it got away

lost another poem
in this computer.
it's like reeling in
a fish
and then it
escapes the hook
just as you reach
for it.

only this poem
wasn't a very big
fish.
the world won't
miss it.
it has swum
away to the
Netherlands.

and I'm baiting
my hook
again.
waiting for
the big
one.

after decades and decades of poverty
as I now approach the lip of the
grave,
suddenly I have a home, a new car, a
spa, a swimming pool, a computer.

will this destroy me?
well, something is bound to destroy
me soon enough.

the boys in the jails, the slaughterhouses,
the factories, on the park benches, in the
post offices, the bars
would never believe me
now.

I have a problem believing myself.
I am no different now
than I was in the tiny rooms of
starvation and madness.
the only difference
is that I am
older.
and I drink better
wine.
all the rest is
nonsense,
the luck of the
draw.

a life can change in a tenth of

a second.
or sometimes it can take
70
years.

either peace or happiness,
let it enfold you.

when I was a young man
I felt that these things were
dumb, unsophisticated.
I had bad blood, a twisted
mind, a precarious
upbringing.

I was hard as granite, I
leered at the
sun.
I trusted no man and
especially no
woman.

I was living a hell in
small rooms, I broke
things, smashed things,
walked through glass,
cursed.
I challenged everything,
was continually being
evicted, jailed, in and
out of fights, in and out
of my mind.
women were something
to screw and rail
at, I had no male
friends,

I changed jobs and
cities, I hated holidays,
babies, history,
newspapers, museums,
grandmothers,
marriage, movies,
spiders, garbagemen,
English accents, Spain,
France, Italy, walnuts and
the color
orange.
algebra angered me,
opera sickened me,
Charlie Chaplin was a
fake
and flowers were for
pansies.

peace and happiness
were to me
signs of
inferiority,
tenants of the weak
and
addled
mind.

but as I went on with
my alley fights,
my suicidal years,
my passage through
any number of
women—it gradually
began to occur to
me
that I wasn't different

from the
others, I was the
same.
they were all fulsome
with hatred,
glossed over with petty
grievances,
the men I fought in
alleys had hearts of
stone.
everybody was nudging,
inching, cheating for
some insignificant
advantage,
the lie was the
weapon and the
plot was
empty,
darkness was the
dictator.

cautiously, I allowed
myself to feel good
at times.
I found moments of
peace in cheap
rooms
just staring at the
knobs of some
dresser
or listening to the
rain in the
dark.
the less I needed
the better I
felt.

maybe the other
life had worn me
down.
I no longer found
glamour
in topping somebody
in conversation.
or in mounting the
body of some poor
drunken female
whose life had
slipped away into
sorrow.

I could never accept
life as it was,
I could never gobble
down all its
poisons
but there were parts,
tenuous magic parts
open for the
asking.

I reformulated,
I don't know when,
date, time, all
that
but the change
occurred.
something in me
relaxed, smoothed
out.
I no longer had to
prove that I was a
man,

I didn't have to prove
anything.

I began to see things:
coffee cups lined up
behind a counter in a
cafe.
or a dog walking along
a sidewalk.
or the way the mouse
on my dresser top
stopped there,
really stopped there
with its body,
its ears,
its nose,
it was fixed,
a bit of life
caught within itself
and its eyes looked
at me
and they were
beautiful.
then—it was
gone.

I began to feel good,
I began to feel good
in the worst
situations
and there were plenty
of those.
like say, the boss
behind his desk,
he is going to have
to fire me.

I've missed too many
days.
he is dressed in a
suit, necktie, glasses,
he says, "I am going
to have to let you go."

"it's all right," I tell
him.

he must do what he
must do, he has a
wife, a house, children,
expenses, most probably
a girlfriend.

I am sorry for him.
he is caught.

I walk out into the blazing
sunshine.
the whole day is
mine.
temporarily,
anyhow.

(the whole world is at the
throat of the world,
everybody feels angry,
short-changed, cheated,
everybody is despondent,
disillusioned.)

I welcomed shots of
peace, tattered shards of
happiness.

I embraced that stuff
like the hottest number,
like high heels, breasts,
singing, the
works.

(don't get me wrong,
there is such a thing as
a cockeyed optimism
that overlooks all
basic problems just for
the sake of
itself—
this is a shield and a
sickness.)

the knife got near my
throat again,
I almost turned on the
gas
again
but when the good
moments arrived
again
I didn't fight them off
like an alley
adversary.
I let them take me,
I luxuriated in them,
I bade them welcome
home.

I even looked into
the mirror
once having thought
myself to be

ugly,
I now liked what
I saw, almost
handsome, yes,
a bit ripped and
ragged,
scars, lumps,
odd turns,
but all in all,
not too bad,
almost handsome,
better at least than
some of those movie
star faces
like the cheeks of
a baby's
butt.

and finally I discovered
real feelings for
others,
unheralded,
like lately,
like this morning,
as I was leaving
for the track,
I saw my wife in bed,
just the shape of
her head there, covers
pulled high, just the
shape of her
head there
(not forgetting
centuries of the living
and the dead and
the dying,

the pyramids,
Mozart dead
but his music still
there in the
room, weeds growing,
the earth turning,
the toteboard waiting for
me)
I saw the shape of my
wife's head,
she so still,
I ached for her life,
just being there
under the
covers.

I kissed her on the
forehead,
got down the stairway,
got outside,
got into my marvelous
car,
fixed the seatbelt,
backed out the
drive.
feeling warm to
the fingertips,
down to my
foot on the gas
pedal,
I entered the world
once
more,
drove down the
hill
past the houses

full and empty
of
people,
I saw the mailman,
honked,
he waved
back
at
me.

the 13th month

in the November of our hell
the birds still fly
or are murdered by the
cats.
in the November of our hell
the boxers hear the bell
and rise to do
what they must do.
in the November of our hell
in the November of our hell,
December
approaches.
in the November of our hell
I walk down the stairway
an old man now.
I reach the bottom,
walk outside
into a world millions of
years old,
I bend down to pet my cat,
his eyes look into mine
and past the
sun
in the November of our hell,
December coming
for both of us
for all of us.
I leave the cat,
climb into my automobile,
the engine starts,
I go out the driveway

backing carefully,
swing into the street
toward the mass of the
living
in the November of their hell,
December coming,
December coming,
look, look, look,
such effrontery!
can you believe it?

and after December?

what month?
what time?

what?

finis, II

we all falter, give way, want to
toss it in.
the bad days come.
the bad days come more often.
we sit and wait, thinking, it will
pass.
but the day will come when it
will not pass.
it will stay.
you will sit in a garden chair
breathing the thick
air.
and an old cat will come and
lay at your feet.
he will wait with you.
death comes slowly some
times.
sometimes much too
slowly.
you will reach down and
pet the cat.
thinking again of the mad and
drunken
years.

the observer

every time I drove past the hospital
I looked at it and thought, some day
I'll be in there.
and eventually I was in there,
sometimes sitting at this long
narrow window
and watching the cars pass on the
street below, as I once had
done.

it was a stupid window,
I had to sit on two folded blankets so that
I could see out.
they had built the window so that part of
the wooden frame
was eye-height
so you either had to look over or
under it.
so I sat on the blankets and looked
over.
well, the window wasn't stupid,
the designers
were.

so I sat there and watched the cars
pass on the street and I thought,
those lucky sons of bitches don't
know how lucky they
are
just to be dumb and driving through
the air

while I sit here on top of my
years
trapped,
nothing but a face in the window
that nobody ever
saw.

easy, go easy, you can't outlast the mountain,
you've just come back from another
war,
go easy.
they are clamoring for you to do it for them once
again,
let them wait.
sit in the shade, wait for your strength to
return.
you'll know when the time is here.
then you'll arrive
for yourself and for them.
a bright sun.
a new fire.
a new gamble.
but
for now
go easy.
let them wait.
let them watch the new boys, the old
boys
meanwhile, you'll need a day or two
to sharpen the
soul,
musing through these D. H. Lawrence
afternoons,
those horseless days,
these nights of music trickling from the
walls,
this waiting for the fullness and the
charge.

this night

I sit in a chair on the balcony
and drink natural spring
water.
the large palms run down the
hill with their dark
heads.
I can see the lights of this
city, of several
cities.

I sit in this balcony chair
where a high voltage wire runs
down and connects underneath
here
where I can reach out and
touch it.
(we can go very fast around
here.)
I hold a bottle of natural
spring water.
a plane flies high in the
overcast, I can't see him,
he can't see
me.
he is very fast.
I can't catch him but I can
pass him by
stretching out
my hand.

it's a cool summer night.

hell trembles nearby,
stretches.
I sit in this chair.
my 6 cats are
close by.

I lift the bottle of water,
take a large
swallow.

things will be far worse than
they are
now.
and far
better.

I wait.

betting on now

I am old enough to have died several
times and I almost have,
now I drive my car through the sun
and over the freeway and past
Watts and to the racetrack
where the parking lot attendants
and the betting clerks
throw garlands of flowers at
me.
I've reached the pause before the full
stop and they are celebrating
because it just seems proper.
what the hell.
the hair I've lost to chemo-
therapy is slowly growing
back but my feet are numb
and I must concentrate on my
balance.
old and battered, olden
matter,
I am still lucky with the
horses.
the consensus is that I
have a few seasons
left.
you would never believe
that I was once young
with a narrow razor face
and crazy eyes of
gloom.
no matter, I sit at my

table
joking with the waiters.
we know it's a fixed
game.
it's funny, Christ, look
at us:
sitting ducks.
"what are you having?"
asks my waiter.
"oh," I say and
read him something
from the menu.
"o.k.," he says
and walks away
between the earthquake,
the volcano and the
leopard.

decline

sitting naked behind the house,
8 a.m., spreading sesame seed oil
over my body, jesus, have I come
to this?
I once battled in dark alleys for a
laugh,
now I'm not laughing.
I splash myself with oil and wonder,
how many years do you want?
how many days?
my blood is soiled and a dark
angel sits in my brain.
things are made of something and
go to nothing.
I understand the fall of cities, of
nations.
a small plane passes overhead.
I look upward as if it made sense to
look upward.
it's true, the sky has rotted:
it won't be long for any of
us.

the rivers of hell are well
peopled with the living.
this is what I write tonight,
a metallic taste in my mouth,
my wife and 6 cats in this
house, I am so sorry for them
because I am not bright with
life for them.
I had no idea that all this
would come so slowly,
running up from my feet
to my brain,
no trumpets blaring
here, no flags of
victory.
I can't even find the
courage to accept my
fate.
I once felt myself greater
than any trap.
nobody is.
damn it, where has the
music gone?
and myself?
pale as mountain light.
damn it, why?
I would have nobody be
me
now.

your life is your life.
don't let it be clubbed into dank
submission.
be on the watch.
there are ways out.
there is light somewhere.
it may not be much light but
it beats the
darkness.
be on the watch.
the gods will offer you
chances.
know them, take them.
you can't beat death but
you can beat death
in life,
sometimes.
and the more often you
learn to do it,
the more light there will
be.
your life is your life.
know it while you have
it.
you are marvelous
the gods wait to delight
in
you.

a challenge to the dark

shot in the eye
shot in the brain
shot in the ass
shot like a flower in the dance

amazing how death wins hands down
amazing how much credence is given to idiot forms of
life

amazing how laughter has been drowned out
amazing how viciousness is such a constant

I must soon declare my own war on their war
I must hold to my last piece of ground
I must protect the small space I have made that has
allowed me life

my life not their death
my death not their death

this place, this time, now
I vow to the sun
that I will laugh the good laugh once again
in the perfect place of me
forever.

their death not my life.

so now?

the words have come and gone,
I sit ill.
the phone rings, the cats sleep.
Linda vacuums.
I am waiting to live,
waiting to die.

I wish I could ring in some bravery.
it's a lousy fix
but the tree outside doesn't know:
I watch it moving with the wind
in the late afternoon sun.

there's nothing to declare here,
just a waiting.
each faces it alone.

Oh, I was once young,
Oh, I was once unbelievably
young!

Photo: Claude Powell

CHARLES BUKOWSKI is one of America's best-known contemporary writers of poetry and prose and, many would claim, its most influential and imitated poet. He was born in Andernach, Germany to an American soldier father and a German mother in 1920, and brought to the United States at the age of three. He was raised in Los Angeles and lived there for fifty years. He published his first story in 1944 when he was twenty-four and began writing poetry at the age of thirty-five. He died in San Pedro, California on March 9, 1994 at the age of seventy-three, shortly after completing his last novel, *Pulp* (1994).

During his lifetime he published more than forty-five books of poetry and prose, including the novels *Post Office* (1971), *Factotum* (1975), *Women* (1978), *Ham on Rye* (1982), and *Hollywood* (1989). His most recent books are the posthumous editions of *What Matters Most Is How Well You Walk Through the Fire* (1999), *Open All Night: New Poems* (2000), *Beerspit Night and Cursing: The Correspondence of Charles Bukowski & Sheri Martinelli, 1960–1967* (2001) and *The Night Torn Mad with Footsteps: New Poems* (2001).

All of his books have now been published in translation in over a dozen languages and his worldwide popularity remains undiminished. In the years to come Black Sparrow will publish additional volumes of previously uncollected poetry and letters.